"PRISONS MAKE US SAFER"

"PRISONS MAKE US SAFER"

And 20 Other Myths About Mass Incarceration

VICTORIA LAW

BEACON PRESS
BOSTON

BEACON PRESS
Boston, Massachusetts
www.beacon.org

Beacon Press books
are published under the auspices of
the Unitarian Universalist Association of Congregations.

24 23   8 7 6 5 4 3

Some incarcerated people requested that I change their names and other
identifying characteristics to protect their identities and prevent staff retaliation
for speaking up about prison conditions.

This book is printed on acid-free paper that meets the uncoated paper
ANSI/NISO specifications for permanence as revised in 1992.

Text design and composition by Kim Arney

Library of Congress Cataloging-in-Publication Data

Names: Law, Victoria, author.
Title: "Prisons make us safer" : and 20 other myths about mass
    incarceration / Victoria Law.
Description: Boston : Beacon Press, [2020] | Includes bibliographical
    references and index.
Identifiers: LCCN 2020011357 (print) | LCCN 2020011358 (ebook) |
    ISBN 9780807029527 (trade paperback) | ISBN 9780807029626 (ebook)
Subjects: LCSH: Imprisonment. | Criminal justice, Administration of. |
    Public relations. | Prisons. | Crime and criminals.
Classification: LCC HV8705 .L38 2020 (print) | LCC HV8705 (ebook) |
    DDC 365—dc23
LC record available at https://lccn.loc.gov/2020011357
LC ebook record available at https://lccn.loc.gov/2020011358

Contents

A Note on Language

I frequently use the term "jails and prisons" when describing the incarceration of people who have lost their liberty. However, jails and prisons serve two different purposes in the criminal court system: Jails are used to detain people while they are awaiting trial; they are also used for people sentenced to less than twelve or, in some states, eighteen months behind bars. Prisons are used to incarcerate people who have been convicted or pleaded guilty and who have been sentenced to more than one year behind bars.

The term "criminal justice system" refers to the legal system in which people are arrested, prosecuted, and threatened with imprisonment. Advocates, particularly abolitionists, are increasingly rejecting the use of that term, noting that the system does not provide justice; it metes out punishment. They often use the terms "criminal legal system" or "criminal punishment system" instead. In most instances, I've chosen to use the term "criminal legal"—rather than the less accurate but more widely used "criminal justice"—to describe the system. I keep the term "criminal justice reform" to indicate the discussions and promises made by politicians and political candidates.

Throughout this book, I have avoided using the terms that are often used to describe people who are incarcerated—"inmates," "prisoners," "convicts," and "felons"—unless I'm referring to a historical term (such as "county convict"). Eddie Ellis, a former Black Panther who spent twenty-three years in prison and then founded the Center for NuLeadership on Urban Solutions, pointed out that these terms are "devoid of humanness which identify us as 'things' rather than as people." I've eschewed these terms in an effort to emphasize that no matter why someone is incarcerated, each of the 2.3 million people behind bars are, first and foremost, human beings.

"PRISONS MAKE US SAFER"

Introduction

The United States incarcerates significantly more of its residents than any other nation. Though it has only 5 percent of the world's population, with 2.2 million people in jails and prisons, it has nearly 25 percent of the world's prisoners. As shocking as it is, for years, society remained largely silent about the massive increases of people being locked away and about the abhorrent conditions inside jails and prisons.

That's beginning to change. In recent years, mass incarceration has become a frequent topic of news headlines, political debates, and even pop culture. Bolstered by shows like *Orange Is the New Black*, documentaries like Ava DuVernay's *13th* and *When They See Us*, Bryan Stevenson's memoir-turned-biopic *Just Mercy*, and Michelle Alexander's best-seller *The New Jim Crow*, prison issues are no longer relegated to the political sidelines.

The prison population hasn't always been so massive. In 1980 the United States held 501,886 people behind bars.[1] But a combination of "tough on crime" policies and the public's demand for longer and harsher punishments increased the number of people behind bars by a whopping 500 percent over the past forty years to today's 2.2 million incarcerated people. If you add in the number of people on probation or parole, that number rises to nearly seven million (from 1.84 million in 1980).

For women, those numbers rose even more dramatically. Between 1980 and 2014, the number of women behind bars increased 800 percent from 26,378 to 215,332.[2] This increase, as distressing as it is, does not include the additional one million women on probation or parole; nor does it include the unknown number of trans women held in men's jails and prisons.

As of 2018, 698 of every 100,000 people are behind bars in the United States.[3] This explosion is what's become known as "mass incarceration."

Still, what do we need to know when we talk about mass incarceration? Who does it affect and how? How exactly did we get to this point—and how can we reverse it?

Despite the heightened attention to mass incarceration in the last decade, many myths persist—often justifying an expansion of the same policies that caused the explosive growth in the first place. For instance, there's the long-standing myth that jails and prisons are necessary to keep people safe from high rates of crime, but violent crime has actually dropped 51 percent over the past twenty-five years. The persistence of this myth justifies the continuation of policies—and the introduction of new laws—that tear individuals from their homes, families, and communities, causing incalculable harm.

Another commonly held myth, which contradicts the previous one, is that most people in prisons, particularly in women's prisons, are convicted of nonviolent drug offenses. This myth focuses attention on only one aspect of the problem or on one segment of the prison population. Such a narrow focus—to the exclusion of other factors—often leads to proposed solutions that may improve conditions for some but often make them worse for others.

This book is divided into four parts reflecting the larger questions around mass incarceration. Each part addresses one common misconception, using facts, figures, and stories from people who have been directly affected.

Part 1 examines and debunks several persistent myths about the causes behind the prison boom, including the myth that private prison corporations drive mass incarceration. This myth, popular among college students working to divest their schools' holdings from private prison corporations, became a talking point among presidential hopefuls during the 2019 Democratic primary debates, with politicians blaming private prison corporations and promising to curb, if not terminate, their contracts. But this myth conveniently ignores the fact that private prisons hold less than 10 percent of the prison population. In fact, not only does focusing solely on private prisons ignore the underlying causes of mass incarceration but it often results in shifting people from private to government-run facilities, where conditions are just as atrocious and life-threatening.

Part 2 addresses myths that justify incarcerating people in need of social services, such as those with mental illnesses or substance addictions. These myths posit that jails and prisons are providing needed services, such as mental health care and other assistance, which would be unavailable to people otherwise. By positioning incarceration as a means of gaining access to needed services, this myth diverts attention from the lack of funding for similar resources outside of jails and prisons.

Part 3 dives deeper to not only debunk myths but also highlight issues that are often overlooked and invisible in larger discussions. These chapters are intended to introduce these issues to readers who are new to issues of incarceration and also to challenge more informed readers to think more deeply and broadly about who is in prison.

I include chapters that focus on the invisibility of women and trans people, who are often excluded from the larger (and purportedly gender-neutral) discussions about mass incarceration. Their concerns, priorities, and even existence are often forgotten in conversations and writings about mass incarceration, frequently leading to reforms that leave them behind. Even in chapters that do not focus on gender and gender identity, many of the stories highlight women caught in the criminal legal system. The majority of people in US jails, prisons, and immigrant detention centers are men. However, incarcerated women experience all of the same banalities and brutalities as their male counterparts; at the same time, their gender and gender identity adds additional layers of injustice and violence inflicted upon them by the prison system. Centering women's stories and experiences allows for a more expansive discussion on the ways in which mass incarceration destroys individual lives as well as families and communities.

Another chapter focuses on immigrant detention. Technically considered a civil (rather than criminal) commitment, immigrant detention has frequently been omitted from discussions about mass incarceration even though detention conditions mimic the worst horrors and abuses inside jails and prisons.

Even before the nation's prison population began to skyrocket, people—and some government bodies—began to call for an end to incarceration. Some even called for prison abolition—the idea of ending not only prisons but also radically changing societal structures and conditions in order to render imprisonment obsolete. The idea of abolition, once viewed largely as a fringe idea, is now gaining more attention and momentum as more people attempt to examine and address the issue of mass incarceration. One week after I turned in edits for this book, Minneapolis police murdered George Floyd, a fifty-eight-year-old Black man. His murder sparked weeks of protests in all fifty US states and internationally. Accompanying these protests were demands to defund and dismantle the police altogether. Abolition has gone from a radical concept often dismissed as pie-in-the-sky by policymakers and the general public to the starting point in an increasing number of public debates and policy discussions in cities across the US.

Part 4 addresses myths about how mass incarceration can be dismantled. These myths range from a narrow focus on people convicted for nonviolent drug offenses to the moral panic around people convicted of sex offenses and murder. Part 4 also introduces the readers to the concept—and existing practices—of restorative justice and transformative justice.

By debunking commonly held myths, I hope this book will challenge people to move beyond narrow definitions and frameworks and to examine mass incarceration in a larger context and in all its complexity. These myths are particularly pernicious now when the public—and politicians—are more open to considering and implementing criminal justice reform. When these myths guide policy, the reforms that are proposed may improve conditions for some people but often worsen conditions for many others. At the same time, reforms that do not consider the entire picture of mass incarceration often widen the net of criminalization, meaning that more people end up under some sort of state supervision and control.

I draw extensively on the incredible writings of many anti-prison organizers, scholars, and writers. I encourage readers to check the endnotes for more about their work.

———

Throughout the writing of this book, I shared drafts with people incarcerated throughout the country and asked for their feedback. Many did so enthusiastically, pointing out areas they felt needed more exploration and sharing their own experiences of criminalization and mass incarceration. Every person told me that I was welcome to include those experiences in this book (though a few requested pseudonyms to protect the privacy of their family members or to prevent retaliation from prison staff). For every instance in which I included a person's experience or observation, I sent them the draft chapter to review. Given that most people in prison have no access to email, this was a time-consuming process, involving paper letters that wound their way first through the postal system and then the prison mailroom before reaching the incarcerated recipient.[4] Then they would have to respond, a process that might also involve waiting days to buy stamps from the prison's commissary (the sole prison store) before the letter made the reverse journey from prison mailroom and US postal system to my mailbox. But the incarcerated letter writers persisted—and without their efforts, this book might be very different.

PART 1

What Drives the Mass Incarceration Boom? Myths About the Causes of Mass Incarceration

The system of mass incarceration is flawed and not working as designed (or, A brief history).

If we look at the history of prisons in the United States, we can see that the system of mass incarceration isn't merely flawed or broken but is operating as it was designed.

As of 2019, the United States had less than 5 percent of the world's population but 25 percent of its prison population.

That year, 2.2 million people were locked in the country's (adult) jails and prisons. If you add in people locked in juvenile detention, immigrant detention, and military prisons, that number rises to approximately 2.3 million people locked behind bars.

Then there are the people under correctional supervision, which means they're under some form of surveillance and restriction either instead of or in addition to a jail or prison sentence. These forms of supervision include house arrest, electronic monitoring, parole, and probation. Individuals are not locked behind bars, but their movements are narrowly circumscribed and any violation of the myriad rules can result in jail or prison. If you count them, the total number of people under some form of correctional control rises to 6.7 million.[1]

At least 4.9 million people cycle through the nation's 3,163 jails each year.[2] The majority of people in jail have not been convicted.

Some will spend a day or two in jail before being released either on bail, meaning that someone paid money for their release pending trial, or on their own recognizance, meaning that a judge allowed them to go home so long as they promise to return to court. Others remain in jail because they cannot afford to post bail.

How did we get to this point? Some might assume it's because our criminal legal system is broken and in need of repair. But if we look at the history of prisons in the United States, we can see that the system of mass incarceration isn't merely flawed or broken but is operating as it was designed: to sweep society's problems (and people seen as problematic) behind gates and walls where few have to see them.

The modern-day prison is a relatively new phenomenon. Before 1773, people were typically jailed while awaiting judgment; their punishments were generally physical and vicious—floggings, time in the stocks, and executions. In the United States, imprisonment as punishment began with the opening of Philadelphia's Walnut Street Jail in 1773.

At the Walnut Street Jail, groups of people served their sentences confined together in large rooms. There was no pretense at rehabilitation; people were simply held until they finished their sentences, often subject to violence and attacks by people incarcerated alongside them as well as their jailers.

In 1790, the jail added a new cellblock, the Penitentiary House. There, people were held in complete isolation. It was the start of a new model—imprisonment as penitence. Taking its name from its mission, the penitentiary was designed to inspire (or coerce) penitence in those who broke the law. People were locked alone in cells for twenty-four hours each day with no human contact, ostensibly to reflect on and repent their criminal actions.

In 1829, Pennsylvania opened the 250-cell Eastern State Penitentiary in Philadelphia. Again, people were held in complete isolation; they were allowed two half-hour stretches per day in a small yard adjoining their cell. These periods were timed so that no two people would be outside at the same time, thus rendering communication impossible. (Cellblocks built in later years eliminated the outside recreation yard.) Inside, the penitentiary's stone walls made it impossible to hear voices from other cells. Not only was the extreme isolation psychologically brutal, but guards also devised physical punishments, including the Iron Gag—a device clamped onto the tongue while a person's arms were crossed and chained behind the neck causing the tongue to tear with any movement—and the water bath, in which guards doused people in cold water and then chained them to a wall for the night.

"I believe that very few men are capable of estimating the immense amount of torture and agony which this dreadful punishment, prolonged for years, inflicts upon the sufferers," wrote novelist Charles Dickens after touring Eastern State in 1842. "I hold this slow and daily tampering with the mysteries of the brain to be immeasurably worse than any torture of the body; and because its ghastly signs and tokens are not so palpable to the eye and sense of touch as scars upon the flesh; because its wounds are not upon the surface, and it extorts few cries that human ears can hear; therefore the more I denounce it, as a secret punishment which slumbering humanity is not roused up to stay."[3]

Eastern State officially abandoned its system of complete isolation in 1913, but the idea of imprisonment as punishment and penance continued—and even spread to countries such as Norway. So too did solitary confinement. To this day, prisons and jails across the US regularly use extended isolation, sometimes for months and years, to further punish people.

After the Civil War, former slave states quickly passed laws regulating and criminalizing certain behaviors—but only for Black people. These Black Codes criminalized a wide range of activities, such as being outside after a certain hour, gathering in small groups, missing work, being perceived as a vagrant, or possessing a firearm. The states also changed the seriousness of an offense; for instance, petty thievery became a felony after large numbers of newly emancipated Black people were forced to steal in order to survive.

These codes changed the color and nature of imprisonment. In Alabama, for instance, 99 percent of prisoners were white before Emancipation. After the Civil War and the state's adoption of the Black Codes, Black people became the majority of people in the penitentiary.[4] In the years following the Civil War, the imprisonment rate for Black people in Mississippi and Georgia rose 300 percent.[5]

The racial underpinnings of criminalization didn't end in the nineteenth century. In the 1960s, as Black people challenged Jim Crow policies throughout the country and images of their protests flickered across the nation's television screens, Richard Nixon, then vice president of the United States, declared that the increase in crime could "be traced directly to the spread of the corrosive doctrine that every citizen possesses an inherent right to decide for himself which laws to obey and when to disobey them."[6] Violent crime did increase during the 1960s, but that wasn't what Nixon was referring to.[7] His fear of "mob rule" was directed at mass sit-ins and civil rights organizing. Policing and imprisonment became tools for incapacitating communities before they could organize and demand social change.

At the same time, criminologists were concluding that prisons did not significantly deter crime and predicted that the prison system would soon fade away. In 1973, the National Advisory Commission on Criminal Justice Standards and Goals found that "the prison, the reformatory and the jail had achieved only a shocking record of failure. There is overwhelming evidence that these institutions create crime rather than prevent it." The commission recommended that "no new institutions for adults should be built and existing institutions for juveniles should be closed."[8]

Lawmakers ignored that recommendation. Instead, aided by the media, they fanned the flames of fear into the conflagration that is now mass incarceration. In the 1980s, President Ronald

Reagan invoked fears of the (Black) crack addict who would rob, rape, and murder for a hit of crack. In 1982, at a time when neither the media nor the general public was concerned about drugs, Reagan launched his war on drugs. But crack cocaine, which became the campaign's main demon, did not hit the streets until three years later.[9] The administration, and later the media, used images and fears of "crack dealers," "crack whores," "crack babies," and "crackheads" to pass harsher laws and more punitive sentences.

It wasn't just Republicans who used these stereotypes to whip up public fears. Democratic senator Joe Biden, who became Barack Obama's vice president and the forty-sixth president, pushed for expanded funding of both police and prisons, shaping the punitive political culture of the 1980s and 1990s. He cowrote and cosponsored the 1986 and 1988 Anti-Drug Abuse Acts, which lengthened sentences for many offenses, provided funding for an escalating drug war, and created the 100-to-1 sentencing disparity in which distribution of five grams of crack cocaine mandated a five-year federal prison sentence. In contrast, distribution of five hundred grams of powder cocaine carried the same five-year sentence.[10]

In 1996, Hillary Clinton, then First Lady, popularized the term "superpredators." She wasn't talking about serial killers or rapists; instead, she was referring to African American youth. "We need to take these people on, they are often connected to big drug cartels, they are not just gangs of kids anymore. They are often the kinds of kids that are called superpredators. No conscience. No empathy. We can talk about why they ended up that way, but first, we have to bring them to heel," she said while campaigning in New Hampshire for her husband's reelection.[11]

These stereotypes have had widespread and long-standing implications. According to the Innocence Project, an organization that works with people who are falsely convicted and imprisoned, 88 percent of their clients who were arrested as minors and later exonerated through DNA evidence are Black; the majority were tried as adults. Overall, 62 percent of their clients exonerated through DNA evidence are Black; 33 percent who were coerced into false confessions were eighteen years old or younger at the time of arrest.[12]

The build-up of prisons and incarceration did not actually curb violent crime, which had already been dropping. Since 1991, violent crime has fallen 51 percent.[13]

But neither Senator Biden nor President Clinton seemed to have gotten the memo about the decade's declining crime rates. Biden authored the 1994 Violent Crime Control and Law Enforcement Act, which provided funding for one hundred thousand new police officers, earmarked $9.7 billion for prisons, created sixty new death penalty offenses, and imposed lengthier prison sentences, including the "Three Strikes, You're Out" provision for a number of federal crimes.

Upon signing it into law, Clinton stated, "Gangs and drugs have taken over our streets and undermined our schools. Every day, we read about somebody else who has literally gotten away with murder."[14]

Once the act became law, twenty-eight states and the District of Columbia jumped on the promise of federal money in exchange for harsher prison terms, enacting stricter sentencing laws for violent crimes.

In the twenty-first century, however, public sentiment is changing. President Barack Obama tweeted, "Mass incarceration makes our entire country worse off, and we need to do something about it."[15] During his presidency, he visited a federal prison and met with people confined inside; reduced sentencing disparities between crack and powder cocaine; and commuted the sentences of 1,715 people, granting them an early release from federal prison.[16] Politicians on both sides of the political spectrum began to shift their rhetoric from "tough on crime" to "smart on crime," acknowledging that previous approaches of locking people up for lengthy periods of time for violating the law have not worked.

At the same time, politicians have seized on—and inflated—public fears of terrorism to fuel the expansion of law enforcement, prosecution, and imprisonment of Muslims living within the United States. Six weeks after 9/11, Congress passed the USA Patriot Act, increasing law enforcement capability and reach. In the ensuing months, thousands of Muslim households were raided; many men were deported or detained for months without charge. By 2004 an estimated one hundred thousand Muslims in the US had experienced at least one of the security measures enabled by the Patriot Act, such as arbitrary arrest, secret and indefinite detention, closed hearings, use of secret evidence, wiretapping, visits from the FBI, and mandatory special registration.[17] However, current discussions about mass incarceration and criminal legal reform frequently exclude mention of these laws—and their widespread violation of civil and human rights under the guise of fighting terrorism.

In 2019, criminal justice reform became a platform for several of the leading Democratic presidential contenders who unveiled platforms to end mass incarceration and linked the issue to other social and economic issues.[18]

Even President Donald Trump jumped on the bandwagon of criminal justice reform. While calling for greater policing, criminalization, and criminal penalties—as well as increased detention and deportation of immigrants—he also championed and signed into law the First Step Act, which shortened mandatory sentences for nonviolent drug convictions and changed the third sentence of a federal three-strikes law from life imprisonment to twenty-five years. (These sentencing reductions were not retroactive; thousands remain behind bars based on past—and now obsolete—sentencing guidelines.)

It's important to understand that these changes are not occurring on their own. Public opinion is shifting because of decades of organizing that has taken many forms. Advocates, including currently and formerly incarcerated people and their loved ones, are challenging and, in some instances, overturning draconian laws.

They've also been fighting to improve jail and prison conditions. In a growing number of instances, their organizing also challenges the bedrock idea that imprisonment is the only solution to societal ills.

Though public opinion—and some public policy—has slowly shifted, mass incarceration remains a method of racialized social control, sweeping those who have been marginalized by societal inequities behind bars and walls rather than addressing these issues. As former political prisoner and renowned prison abolitionist Angela Davis wrote, "The prison has become a black hole into which the detritus of contemporary capitalism is deposited."[19] The focus on locking people up continually redirects society's focus (and resources) from the need for employment, housing, comprehensive medical and mental health care, quality education, and violence prevention.

CHAPTER 2

We need prisons to make us safer.

*Americans have been sold the story—lock 'em up and
you're safe. But you create a more damaged person.*

—KAMADIA, imprisoned in Texas since 2007

The United States now has 2.3 million people behind bars of
some form or another. These are not 2.3 million isolated individuals—their imprisonment sends reverberations into their families and communities. On any given day, 2.7 million children have
a parent in prison. Incarcerating that parent removes a source of
financial and emotional support for both children and adult family
members. For families who are already in economically precari-
ous situations, removing a parent can plunge them into poverty,
reduce their safety, and make them more vulnerable to arrest and
incarceration.

This is not to say that we don't need interventions when harm
and violence happen. But prisons have proven again and again to be
an ineffective intervention. First, we must remember that incarceration is a form of punishment and incapacitation that happens
after harm has occurred, not before. We must also remember that
incarceration addresses only certain types of harm. People who
sell drugs on the street risk arrest and imprisonment. But the same
rarely applies to wealthy people like the Sackler family, who earned
billions from OxyContin, the addictive painkiller launched in 1996
that spawned today's opioid crisis.[1] Likewise, board members and

corporate executives responsible for oil spills and other environmental disasters or for precipitating economic crises rarely face handcuffs and jail time.

So when confronted with the statement that prisons provide safety, we should ask, Safety for whom? And from what?

The three main arguments in support of incarceration boil down to deterrence, incapacitation, and justice for victims.

If we focus solely on interpersonal crime and harm, we might believe that the threat of imprisonment deters crime and wrongdoing. But with 2.3 million people behind bars, we can see that deterrence actually isn't happening.

Danielle Sered is the founder and director of Common Justice, a program that promotes alternatives to incarceration and provides services to victims. Based in New York City, the program works with young adults facing violent felony charges, including assault and robbery, and their victims.[2]

Sered recalled posing a question to the program's youths, all of whom had been incarcerated. As you were committing the crime, she asked them, what penalty did you think you would receive if caught? Their answers debunk the theory that the threat of incarceration deters people from committing crime: one-third did not think of a penalty at all. Another third thought the penalty would be substantially less. The final third thought they might face a far greater penalty if caught but, at the time they committed the acts, were indifferent to the potential consequences.[3] In other words, the threat of prison was no deterrent to their decision.

But what about incapacitating people who commit harm? Imprisonment does incapacitate a person, but it also rips people away from their families and communities, placing them in environments rife with chaos, abuse, and violence.

"Americans have been sold the story—lock 'em up and you're safe," reflected Kamadia, a former nurse, who has been imprisoned in Texas since 2007. "But you create a more damaged person. The first lesson I learned in prison [was] don't trust anyone.

Don't show emotions. I scare myself with how desensitized I have become to suicide and rape. I often ask, 'Where's the empathetic nurse?' Gone."[4]

She's referring to the often torturous conditions inside jails and prisons. These conditions include physical assaults, verbal taunts, and sexual abuse—from prison staff and other incarcerated people. They also include inaccessible and often inadequate medical and mental health care, which often exacerbates a person's preexisting conditions. They include practices like solitary confinement, or locking a person in a cell with no human contact for at least twenty-three hours each day; in some states, people have been locked in solitary for months, years, and sometimes decades, creating and exacerbating post-traumatic stress disorder and other mental health conditions. For those lucky enough to receive visits from family and loved ones, conditions include submitting to a strip search before and after each visit. In 2020, these conditions became potentially deadly as crowded jails and prisons became petri dishes for the novel coronavirus, or COVID-19. The Centers for Disease Control and Prevention (CDC) recommended preventive measures of social distancing of at least six feet and frequent handwashing, both of which are nearly impossible behind bars. In many jails and prisons, people sleep less than two feet apart from one another and are moved in groups around the facility. During non-pandemic times, soap is strictly rationed and, even with threats of rampant coronavirus spread, many jails and prisons failed to provide adequate soap or handwashing facilities.

Meanwhile, rehabilitative programs, including counseling, effective drug treatment, and educational and vocational programs, are often scarce, leaving many with little to do. (During the coronavirus crisis, even these scarce programs were canceled.)

Even without a life-threatening pandemic, research has shown that incarceration is associated with an *increase* in recidivism, or committing a new crime, especially when compared to non-prison consequences, such as probation.[5] The Department of Justice found that 83 percent (or five out of six) people leaving state prison were arrested within nine years of their release.[6] The report did not list the most common reasons for arrest, though it did note that people initially imprisoned for a property conviction were more likely to be arrested again than those incarcerated for a violent crime.[7]

Imprisonment not only disrupts the individual person's life but also pulls them out of their roles in their family and community. Children lose a parent; families lose a member who had helped with the bills, caregiving, and general support of the household. Those relationships tend to fray over time, particularly with lengthy incarcerations, making it less likely that the person will be able to pick up the pieces of their life upon release. In addition, a prison record can impede people from finding a job, securing housing, or being accepted to college.

In contrast, reducing prison populations seems to be correlated with a reduction in crime. While the nation's prison population ballooned again and again throughout the 1990s until 2015, some states started reducing their prison populations during that period. Contrary to fear-based myths, these states have not seen an increase in crime. In fact, they've seen the opposite. In New York, the combined jail and prison incarceration rate was cut by 55 percent between 1994 and 2014; during those twenty years, the rate of serious crime in New York City fell 58 percent.[8] New Jersey reduced its prison population by 25 percent, and reports of violent crime dropped by 31 percent. California reduced its prison population by 25 percent while reports of violent crime dropped 21 percent.[9] In Chicago, the number of people sentenced to prison or jail decreased 19 percent between 2017 and 2018; violent crime dropped 8 percent during that same period.[10]

Cincinnati illustrates how decreased incarceration does not decrease safety. In 2008, the city shuttered its 822-bed Queensgate Correctional Facility, eliminating one-third of Cincinnati's jail beds. When the closure was announced, critics feared a spike in crime. In fact, the reverse happened. With jail beds reduced from

2,300 to 1,500, police were forced to undergo a paradigm shift: they began viewing arrests as a limited commodity rather than the standard response. Between 2008 to 2014, felony arrests decreased 41.3 percent; misdemeanor arrests dropped 32.7 percent.

The decrease in arrests wasn't because police were ignoring violence and harm. Instead, the decrease reflected a dropping crime rate. During that same period, the city's violent crime fell 38.5 percent while property crime decreased 18.9 percent. The decrease in arrests also reflected a shift in priorities, forcing police officers to focus on actions that actually threatened public safety rather than minor legal infractions.[11]

New York City shows a different story: despite the dramatic decrease in homicides and violent crime between 1994 and 2014, the city continues to add more officers to the police force, and those police officers continue arresting people for minor violations. In 2018, police made 808 arrests for rape. In contrast, they made over five thousand arrests for fare evasion.[12] These arrests don't contribute to public safety; instead, they punish people who cannot afford to pay $2.75 for a subway or bus ride, subjecting them to arrest, a fine that is thirty times greater than the fare they could not afford, and the threat of jail. When COVID-19 hit the United States, New York City became the epicenter of the epidemic, and its jail system became its flashpoint. By May 2020, the jails' rate of infection was 9.53 percent, more than double its 4.1 percent infection rate on April 1. In contrast, the infection rate of New York City's general population was 2.15 percent in early May and 0.5 percent on April 1.[13]

The war on terror is another illustration of how incarceration not only fails to keep individuals and communities safe but also manufactures crime. Under the mantle of fighting terrorism, federal authorities have used material support bans (first introduced in 1996 by the Antiterrorism and Effective Death Penalty Act) to expand their criminalization of Muslims for acts such as translating websites, allowing friends to store belongings in their apartment, and lending money for plane tickets, leading to decades-long prison sentences. Like the Black Codes in the post–Civil War South, material support bans only apply to Muslims; similar actions conducted by non-Muslims are not surveilled or criminalized. At the same time, federal authorities have also used its web of over fifteen thousand paid informants to entrap other Muslims in fake terror plots, leading to splashy arrests and lengthy prison sentences.[14] But these acts have not kept individuals or communities safe from violence or terror; instead, they inflict violence and terror on immigrant and Muslim families and communities while justifying continual increases in law enforcement and prison budgets.

If incarceration actually doesn't keep us safe by deterring or incapacitating people who cause harm, why then do we continue to think that prisons keep us safe?

The media plays a significant role in reinforcing and perpetuating this myth.

Since 1991, violent crime in the United States has fallen more than 51 percent. Between 1990 and 1998, the nation's homicide rates dropped by half. But the average American wouldn't have known that. During those eight years, homicide stories on three major news networks rose nearly four times, fueling fears of murderous crime waves.[15]

At the same time, the number of people behind bars increased dramatically. In 1990, 771,243 people were in state or federal prisons. It was a figure that the Bureau of Justice Statistics, the federal agency that tracks imprisonment numbers, called "a record high."[16] Throw in the 405,320 people in local jails and the nation had nearly 1.2 million people behind bars that year.[17]

If imprisonment acted as a deterrent or a form of incapacitation, then that record high should have made Americans safe. Instead, it was eclipsed again and again in subsequent years. Over 1.5 million people were in jails and prisons by 1995.[18] By 2000, nearly two million were in prisons or jails.[19] By 2007, that number had soared to nearly 2.3 million.[20]

One might assume that the decrease in homicide and other violence is due to rising incarceration. But this actually is not a cause-and-effect relationship. Again, it's important to remember that incarceration is a form of punishment and incapacitation that typically happens *after* harm has occurred, not before.

That leads to the third argument: doesn't incarceration provide justice for victims? That argument also falls short when looking at reality.

First, over half (or 52 percent) of violent crimes in the United States go unreported.[21] Of those, fewer than half result in an arrest. Fewer than half of those arrests result in conviction.[22] This means that incarceration addresses less than one-quarter of harmful instances in which there is a victim. Furthermore, many victims come from the same communities and often the same demographics as those who have harmed them. They may not want to see their relatives, neighbors, or community members locked away; instead, they may want an end to the harm, an acknowledgment and apology about the harm that was caused, and efforts to ensure that the person will not repeat their harmful actions.[23] But this is not something that incarceration can provide, a reality recognized by many victims, particularly those in marginalized communities and those harmed by loved ones.

For those who do turn to the criminal legal system, they find that, beyond allowing them to testify in court and giving them the opportunity to give a victim impact statement, incarceration does not provide sustained resources for healing.

In contrast, restorative justice is a process that involves not only the person who was harmed and the person who did the harm but also people who have been indirectly affected, such as family members, neighbors, and community members. They come together to identify and address the harm and also the needs and obligations required to begin the process of healing and accountability. In contrast to the criminal legal system, many restorative justice programs do not label participants as "victims" or "perpetrators," as if one act or set of actions defines their entire identity. Instead, they are often referred to as "the person who was harmed" and "the person who did the harm."

In New York City, Common Justice staff work with both parties to address the harm and its resulting consequences. The process takes months—and at the end, both parties sit down and meet. The victim talks about the effects of the crime on their lives and their well-being; they also talk about what they need from the person who caused that harm. The person who caused the harm listens and agrees to these terms.

Given these realities, we should question whether incarceration truly keeps us safe from harm and violence or whether this is a myth that diverts attention and political will away from the resources that do keep society safe—housing, education, well-paying and fulfilling jobs, comprehensive medical and mental health care, violence prevention, community cohesion, and less criminalization.

CHAPTER 3

Prisons are places of rehabilitation.

Society thinks people enter prison and leave
better. But it's the opposite.

—KAMADIA, imprisoned in Texas since 2007

The first time Mwalimu Shakur was sent to juvenile detention, he was twelve years old and had been found guilty of robbery. Six months later, he was released to his grandmother's house in Los Angeles.

"Nothing had changed in those six months," he recalled. His four cousins were still gang members running the streets. "When we were at my grandmother's, we talked about what we were doing, learning how to sell drugs, burglaries and shoot dice and guns." Four years later, he and his cousin were caught burglarizing a department store. Shakur was sent back to juvenile detention, this time for a year. He spent that year exercising, writing letters to his family and girlfriends, and talking with the friends he made there.

Looking back, Shakur, now forty-six, reflected, "I always thought that breaking the law was how you made it in the ghetto. I was too young to get a job and besides, if you didn't have any family who owned a small business, you weren't gonna find work. Crime is what I was being taught by my older homies. It was how we survived."[1]

Five years after that second incarceration, Shakur was imprisoned again, this time as an adult in California's prison system. At one prison, a riot broke out. "Since this was my first prison sentence, I had to get involved as the older cats expect youngsters to put in work," he explained. Being "put to work" meant stabbing members of other gangs, and for the next nine months Shakur ended up in administrative segregation (the prison's term for solitary confinement, in which a person spends twenty-three hours a day locked in a cell).[2] But those months in isolation did nothing to rehabilitate Shakur. When he was released from solitary, he attacked another man and was sent back to segregation, this time for sixteen months.[3] That was when some of the older Black men encouraged him to read Malcolm X, Marcus Garvey, the Black Panthers, and George Jackson. He did and began to change his thinking. Shakur is quick to note that it wasn't the prison that encouraged this change. Had he not encountered these mentors, he might have continued on the same destructive path.

Shakur's experience raises the questions: What does it mean to rehabilitate a person to their former state if that state involves poverty, racism, unemployment, unstable housing, and/or violence? Can a person be rehabilitated if they have never been habilitated (or made fit or capable for society)?

Many people believe that prisons are sites of rehabilitation. In reality, however, rehabilitative opportunities in prison are few and far between.

Numerous studies have shown that the best form of rehabilitation in prison is education. Approximately 60 percent of people entering prisons lack high school diplomas or GEDs. While in prison, they may be able to enroll in GED classes, but that's typically where their formal education stops.

It wasn't always this way. In 1994, the US had 350 college-in-prison programs, largely funded by Pell Grants, or noncompetitive need-based federal funding. Pell Grants for people in prison accounted for 0.1 percent of the federal grants' annual budget. In other words, these grants did not take financial aid away from nonincarcerated college students. In addition, rates of recidivism dropped more than 40 percent among those who had enrolled in educational programs while incarcerated.[4]

But accompanying the rise of tough-on-crime policies and mass incarceration in the 1980s and 1990s came demands to make prisons more severe. Conservative politicians like North Carolina senator Jesse Helms stoked outrage that people in prison might be able to enroll in college courses while the cost of higher education remained out of reach for many "law-abiding citizens." The question could have been why college tuition was so expensive in the first place, but his focus was on why people who had been convicted of crimes might benefit during their time behind bars.

The 1994 Violent Crime Control and Law Enforcement Act cut Pell Grants for people in prison. The move defunded all but eight of the country's college-in-prison programs. Two decades later, in 2015, the Obama administration announced a pilot program to fund sixty-seven colleges to offer courses to approximately twelve thousand people in prisons.[5] That year, over 1.5 million people were in state and federal prisons across the country.[6] In other words, less than 1 percent of the nation's prison population has been able to participate in this modest program.

Now even basic education can be hard to obtain within prisons. In 2020, the Bureau of Prisons announced that 16,400 people were on the waiting list for the federal prisons' literacy programs.[7]

Prisons generally offer self-help programs, but many students who have participated report they're often useless. In Texas, Kamadia enrolled in classes that ostensibly addressed toxic relationships, anger management, and bridges to life. She didn't think these classes would rehabilitate her but was hoping they would increase her chances of parole. "I got *nothing* out of the classes," she recalled with frustration. Unbelievably, the class that focused on parenting consisted mostly of coloring. The anger management class encouraged women to rip pages out of a book and count to ten when they felt angry, but it never encouraged students to explore the underlying violence and trauma behind their anger.[8]

Even if the classes did encourage participants to talk about their own experiences, the programs' group setting prevented them from sharing, let alone exploring, their past traumas.

"You can't expose yourself within a group," Kamadia explained. "You can't look weak." If a woman talked about past violence or trauma, other participants would verbally gang up on her. Kamadia recalled that during a domestic violence class, one of her friends talked about being molested as a child and its continued impact on her decision-making as an adult.

"The truth is, I could more than relate," Kamadia wrote. But knowing how a person's past hardships—perceived as weaknesses by those incarcerated—would be used against her in nearly every future prison interaction, she refrained from commiserating. Instead, she recalled, "I did what everyone in the group did. We attacked—verbally." Rather than helping the woman process her trauma, they belittled her for her past experience and for failing to be a strong Black woman—each woman trying to be more vicious than the next.[9]

Jack, who is also incarcerated in Texas, has an even more jaundiced view of the rehabilitative quality of prison programs. In 2001, he enrolled in the prison's computer maintenance class. "I was extremely excited to learn the technical aspects of computers and believed I was learning a skill which would be in great demand," he recalled. The instructor encouraged Jack to take the certification test. "I've never been much of a test taker. I freeze up and flunk every time," he explained. "But this time I was determined to prevail." Jack asked his parents, whose only income was from social security, to cover the hundred-dollar test fee. "This was a great sacrifice, but they paid it as an investment in my future."

Jack passed the test and received his certificate. But on release in 2002, he learned that those skills were outdated. All of the time, energy, and money that he and his family had poured into his education—as well as their hopes for a better future—were for nothing.[10]

Other prisons have long waiting lists for the handful of educational programs offered. Some, like the perpetually overcrowded Mabel Bassett Correctional Center in Oklahoma, limit participation to people nearing the end of their sentences. Hazel, who has served eight years of an eighteen-year sentence, notes that these constraints exclude those in the middle of long sentences, like herself, as well as those serving life or life without parole sentences.[11]

Then there's the question of whether rehabilitation can take place in an environment rife with violence, drugs, and chaos. In jails and prisons, security is always a priority. That means whenever a fight or other security issue arises, programs can be abruptly canceled.

Even when violence is not a pervasive threat, substandard living conditions can impede attempts at personal progress. Take the Central Mississippi Correctional Facility, for example. The prison incarcerates over 3,800 men and women who are separated by gender and confined to their own housing units, yards, and recreational areas.[12] What this means, noted Emma, who has been incarcerated there for the past several years, is that women are often shuffled around to accommodate the larger male prison population.

In January 2018, the prison moved 140 women into a housing unit that had previously been condemned and closed. It was unclear what renovations had been made to bring the building up to code, as the unit had only six toilets, eight sinks, six showers, and two water fountains with water that, at best, was "tepid." Mold grew on the walls.[13]

The move was part of Mississippi's attempts to juggle its prison population, particularly the growing number of women in custody. In 2018, the state's incarceration rate was 161 of every 100,000 women. In contrast, the national rate was 133 of every 100,000 women.[14] But the growing number of women sentenced to prison weren't being offered rehabilitation; instead, they were crammed into substandard living conditions where they were expected to quietly serve their sentences.

"Society thinks people enter prison and leave better," reflected Kamadia. "But it's the opposite. I was an extrovert—ambitious, outdoor-loving person. Now I'm not comfortable with crowds, I'm constantly looking over my shoulder, assessing my situation."[15] Instead of rehabilitating her, imprisonment has turned the former Catholic schoolgirl, raised on ideals of helping and trusting others, into someone who instinctively distrusts any gestures of kindness. "I refuse a Kleenex if I have a runny nose," she explained. "Reflexively, I think, what does this person want from me? Why would they give me this? Why are they being nice?" Her childhood teachings of helping others in need have been replaced by the prison's lesson of remaining silent in the face of injustice and violence. "I've allowed this place to steal my voice and my choice," she reflected.[16]

That's the same for Mary Fish, who credits prison for teaching her how to hustle. When Fish entered prison in 1982, her family was unable to send her money that would allow her to buy any of the necessities—such as soap, feminine hygiene products, or snacks—that would help her through her ten-year sentence. She spent the first five years working in the prison kitchen, where she learned to stuff food down her bra or pants and later use it to barter with women whose families did send them money.

Another woman introduced her to a more lucrative hustle—writing to lonely men outside of the prison. "I had always loved to write, so it became easy to get money orders in from the men I wrote," Fish recalled. "I learned to lie really well in those letters. I wrote several men and I told each one I loved them. I began to have new televisions, new comforters, new clothes ordered from Spiegel, canteen every week, money on my books."[17]

Stories like these are the norm, not the exception. Why, then, does the myth of prisons as sites of rehabilitation continue? Perhaps it's because incarceration was conceived as a form of rehabilitation. Prisons in earlier centuries were often temporary holding cells for people awaiting trial, punishment, or execution. In the eighteenth century, the Quakers introduced what would become the nation's modern-day prisons as alternatives to the brutal punishments for crimes. Instead of the stocks, floggings, or the gallows, the Quakers envisioned a penitentiary in which the convicted person, or penitent, would be confined in isolation to reflect on their crimes and repent.

Imprisonment as reform wasn't limited to people who committed crimes. It also extended to those who deviated from social norms. At the end of the nineteenth century, as women began leaving home and asserting their independence, reformatories were created specifically for women who did not acquiesce to conservative social norms. Women were sent to reformatories for drunkenness, premarital or extramarital sex, or any other act in which they asserted their independence. Men were not subjected to incarceration for these actions; there were no men's reformatories.

The reformatories purported to "reform" these wayward women into model housewives and mothers, teaching them the domestic arts. At the same time, these institutions were places of torture, severely punishing women for what was considered rude behavior, including masturbation. Punishments included beatings, knocking women's heads against walls, hosing them down, denying them access to water closets (toilets), and "ducking" them in cold water (a nineteenth-century version of waterboarding).[18] In 1881, an Indiana legislative committee conducted an investigation into rumors of abuse within its reformatory. They found that women had been subjected to prolonged isolation, physical and sexual abuse, water torture, food and clothing deprivation, forced abortions, and unwarranted surgical operations and experimentations. All of these tortures occurred within the walls of a reformatory that had been widely applauded as a gender-responsive institution to rehabilitate women. Being a reformatory didn't curb the abuses; it enabled them.[19]

While reformatories ended in the 1930s in the United States, the myth of prisons as sites of rehabilitation persists.

Finally, it's important to think about the idea of rehabilitation. Merriam-Webster's dictionary defines *rehabilitation* as the act of restoring something (or in this case, someone) to their former capacity. But what does that mean for the majority of people who end up behind bars?

Mary Fish's former capacity was as a Native American woman and underemployed single mother in Oklahoma, a state with scant resources to help people lift themselves out of poverty. Her life was shaped not only by poverty but also by family and domestic violence, racism, sexism, and a lack of educational opportunities, despite her consistently acing tests at school.

Similarly, Mwalimu Shakur's trajectory was shaped by living in a community in which gangs and crime were the dominant economic opportunity.

Writing from an Oklahoma prison, where she has spent eight years watching women cycle in and out of prison, Hazel reflects, "The problem begins in society where the disenfranchised are regularly ignored, marginalized and oppressed by the systems that fail them as human beings. They are then caught in the cycles of poverty, addiction, violence and hopelessness that they came from or are graduated into the system of state custody or prison."

Prison cannot address these systemic failings. They can only cover them up.

CHAPTER 4

Private prison corporations drive mass incarceration.

Ending a prison contract does not relieve anybody who's locked up of one minute of time that they owe to the building.

—RUTH WILSON GILMORE

As mass incarceration enters public awareness and garners more attention and outrage, private prison corporations are frequently blamed for the boom in imprisonment.

In reality, privately run prisons incarcerate between 8 and 8.5 percent of the US prison population.[1] Over 90 percent of US prisons are owned and operated by the government. Some are run by the Federal Bureau of Prisons, while the vast majority are operated by state governments.

Private prisons are owned and operated by corporations as a privately contracted public service. There are two ways in which these corporations contract with and are paid by the government. One is through a per-diem rate in which the corporation is paid a fixed fee for each person per day. The other is through a contracted rate, regardless of the numbers of people who are sent to that prison. But more than half of these contracts contain occupancy guarantees (often called a "lock-up quota" by advocates), in which a state guarantees to pay for a set number of people, even if there aren't that many people in custody. These quotas range between 80 and 100 percent occupancy in most private prison contracts.[2]

At the end of 2018, private prisons had incarcerated 118,444 people, or 8 percent of all state and federal prisoners, a 2 percent decrease from the previous year.[3] Private prisons have, however, expanded to confine 73 percent of people in immigrant detention. Immigrant detention is considered a form of civil, not criminal confinement, though conditions in immigrant detention and prisons are alarmingly similar.

Private prisons were created to capitalize on the trend of mass criminalization, incarceration, and detention—or the need to put the ever-increasing number of people somewhere. They were not the driving force behind these ballooning numbers.

Incarceration, spurred by racialized fears of crime and violence, had already been on the rise in the 1980s when two of the largest private prison corporations were created.

———

In 1983, the Corrections Corporation of America (now CoreCivic) was founded. That year, approximately 24,000 people were sent to state and federal prisons, bringing the total number of prisoners to 438,830.[4] It was a 12 percent increase from the previous year's prison population (414,362 people) and more than double the 229,721 prisoners in 1974.

Two years later, in 1985, CCA's main competitor, Wackenhut (now called GEO Group) was formed. These two corporations have since become the giants of the private prison and detention industry, though they remain dwarfed by the larger systems of publicly managed prisons and jails.

The myth that private prisons drive mass incarceration has fueled divestment campaigns pushing universities and pension funds to divest their investments from private prison corporations.

Divestment campaigns have also targeted banks that provide financing to these corporations. Both CoreCivic and GEO Group are set up as real estate investment trusts, which allows them to avoid taxes but requires them to distribute 90 percent of their profits to shareholders. Thus, they rely on bank financing for daily operations and expansions.

In March 2019, divestment campaigners celebrated when JP Morgan Chase, which had provided at least $254 million in debt financing to the two largest private prison corporations, announced that it would not provide new financing to the private prison industry."[5] Since then, eight banks have followed suit, though they still honor (and have extended) already existing financing contracts.[6]

In late 2019, California passed Assembly Bill 32, which prevents the state from entering into or renewing contracts with for-profit prison companies after January 1, 2020; the bill also phases out private facilities by 2028. The law does not extend to privately run federal prisons and city jails. It also does not require that people currently held in private prisons or detention centers be released.[7]

While these victories are significant financial blows to private corporations that profit from caging people, they do not end mass incarceration.[8] No one in prison (or in immigrant detention) will go home as a result of these divestments. Meanwhile, existing (and proposed new) legislation continues to send people to jails, prisons, and immigrant detention centers.

This is not to say that these corporations don't work to expand imprisonment—and their profits. They have spent tens of millions of dollars in lobbying not only to keep and grow their businesses but also to advocate for punitive laws that would lock people up for longer periods of time. GEO Group, the nation's largest private prison corporation, spent $2.5 million on lobbying between 2004 and 2012; the Corrections Corporation of America (now Core-Civic), the second-largest private prison corporation, spent $17.4 million on lobbying between 2002 and 2012.[9] In 2016, GEO Group spent $3.3 million in lobbying while CoreCivic spent $1.8 million.[10] Both have spent millions in political contributions as well.

But these contributions to individual lawmakers are often dwarfed by those from public sector unions, which represent guards working in government-run jails and prisons. In 1998, for instance, private prison corporations contributed $285,996 to both Democratic and Republican campaigns. In contrast, the California Correctional Peace Officers Association (CCPOA), the union for California's thirty-one thousand state prison guards, contributed nearly $2.2 million.[11] Politicians understand that, unlike private prison corporations, unions also deliver votes.

Focusing on private prisons also obscures the role of an even more powerful interest group and lobby—prison guard associations and unions.[12]

In the early 1990s, concerned that private prisons threatened public prison jobs, the Florida Police Benevolent Association created the Private Corrections Institute (now called the Private Corrections Working Group), which advocated against the privatization of incarceration. The institute developed the messaging that privatization led to more escapes, poor medical and rehab services, and increased violence in the prisons. What the institute did not acknowledge is that these issues also plagued (and continue to plague) publicly run prisons.[13]

CCPOA is considered one of the most powerful political unions in California, and it has supported campaigns for the state's tough-on-crime measures of the 1990s, including the 1994 three-strikes ballot initiative, which resulted in the explosion of California's prison population. It has also contributed millions to electoral candidates, including to the campaigns of Governors Pete Wilson, Gray Davis, and Jerry Brown.[14] CCPOA also holds the promise of delivering over thirty thousand votes.

As of January 2017, California had 35 state prisons and 43 conservation camps that, altogether, incarcerate approximately 129,000 people. Another 9,000 Californians were incarcerated in private prisons either within California or out of state.[15] CCPOA opposes prison privatization, equating it with job loss and an attack on public sector jobs and unions. For years, the union success-fully fought to keep private corporations from operating any of the state's prisons.

Unions representing jail and prison guards have also opposed decarceration measures, understanding that having fewer people incarcerated increases the risk of closing prisons and cutting back on correctional officer jobs. CCPOA spent more than $250,000 on a campaign opposing 2004 revisions to the state's three-strikes law.[16] It also spent one million dollars to kill California's 2008 Proposition 5, which would have increased funding for nonprison diversions for people convicted of nonviolent drug offenses and allowed for time off prison sentences for the completion of prison programs.

The American Federation of State, County, and Municipal Em-ployees (AFSCME) represents eighty-five thousand prison guards nationwide. When advocates began a campaign to close the notori-ous supermax prison in Tamms, Illinois, where people were held in long-term solitary confinement for years, AFSCME Council 31, which represents Illinois prison guards, waged its own campaign, invoking fears for public safety. The union also filed a lawsuit claim-ing that the closure would create harmful working conditions by sending the state's most violent prisoners back to other prisons.[17]

In New York City, the Correction Officers' Benevolent Asso-ciation (COBA), which represents the city's jail guards, has con-demned efforts to close Rikers Island and replace it with four smaller jails that will hold only half the number of people that the city's sprawling island-jail complex currently detains. COBA con-tributed $971,012 to state electoral campaigns between 2009 and 2014.[18] The union for New York's state prison officers, which has opposed reforms to solitary confinement and parole practices, spent nearly $1.2 million between 2009 and 2014.[19]

Finally, and most importantly, as abolitionist and prison scholar Ruth Wilson Gilmore has noted, "Ending a prison contract does not relieve anybody who's locked up of one minute of time that they owe to the building."[20] This was apparent in August 2016 when Obama's deputy attorney general, Sally Yates, instructed federal prison officials not to renew contracts with private prison corporations once they expired.[21] Yates echoed the messaging of the Private Corrections Institute, stating that "time has shown that they compare poorly to our own Bureau facilities. They simply do not provide the same level of correctional services, programs, and resources; they do not save substantially on costs; and as noted in a recent report by the Department's Office of Inspector General, they do not maintain the same level of safety and security."[22] The announcement only pertained to contracts between the Bureau of Prisons and private corporations; contracts with the US immigration and Customs Enforcement (ICE) would not be affected.

While advocates applauded the announcement, some were cautious about what the decision actually meant for people serving federal prison sentences.

Andrea James, a cofounder of the National Council for Incarcerated and Formerly Incarcerated Women and Girls, noted that Yates's memo "doesn't say that they're not going to incarcerate them somewhere else."[23] James spent eighteen months in a prison run by the federal government. There, she witnessed numerous examples of neglect and abuse ranging from the lack of soap in the prison's bathrooms to inadequate and sometimes life-threatening medical care.[24]

James's concern for the well-being of those incarcerated is not unfounded. The fight to eliminate private prisons has resulted in some states, such as Arkansas, Idaho,[25] and Pennsylvania, significantly reducing their use of private prisons, while Kentucky and Wisconsin have canceled their contracts completely. But divestment from private prisons was a victory only in that AFSCME and other unions representing corrections officers defeated private contractors. The people incarcerated in those prisons were then shuffled into state-run prisons; they were not released to their home communities.

In 2017, shortly after Trump's inauguration, the Department of Justice reversed course and stated that it would continue contracting with private corporations for its federal prison system.[26] But the number of people in private (nonimmigrant) prisons continues to hover around 8 percent.[27]

That doesn't mean that these corporations haven't profited from caging people. In the last quarter of 2018, revenue from Core-Civic's prisons and immigrant detention facilities amounted to $436 million; its total revenue for that quarter was $482.2 million.[28] GEO Group's revenue from that same period was $599.4 million.[29]

While not insignificant, these sums pale in comparison to the $11.9 billion that California spent on its state-run prisons in 2018.[30]

Peter Wagner, the cofounder and director of the Prison Policy Initiative, has a useful analogy to keep in mind when considering the role of private prisons in mass incarceration: think of private prisons, he advises, as "less the seed or the fertilizer fueling mass incarceration and more like a parasite on the publicly-owned prison system."[31]

CHAPTER 5

Private corporations and profit from prison labor drive mass incarceration.

Prison labor—and whatever profit it might garner—is a side effect of incarceration, not a driving force.

The Thirteenth Amendment to the Constitution abolishes slavery and involuntary servitude except for those who are "duly convicted" of a crime. This exception has led to the myth that prison labor has replaced slavery and is the driving force behind mass incarceration. It would be a tidy explanation, but it's just not true.

In reality, fewer than half of the 2.3 million people behind bars work while incarcerated. Even fewer work to enrich private corporations: less than 1 percent of these 2.3 million people work for private corporations that have set up shop within the prison.[1]

Then why does this myth persist?

To answer that, we need to look at the nation's history. In 1718 England passed the Transportation Act, allowing the country to send its convicted people to its American colonies as indentured servants to provide cheap labor to merchants and planters for a set amount of time. Nearly sixty thousand people, known as "the King's Passengers," were sent to what later became the United States. Many remained in the colonies past their terms of servitude and began new lives as free people. But until its elimination in 1783 after the American War of Independence, convict labor wasn't tied to race; the people who were leased had descendants who later became categorized as white.[2]

The color of convict leasing dramatically darkened after the Civil War. Southern states capitalized on the Thirteenth Amendment's exception, passing the Black Codes and creating the convict lease system to exploit the labors of newly freed Black people. Crews of prisoners were leased from the state by private companies, performing labor ranging from plantation work in Mississippi to coal mining in Alabama, from railroads in Tennessee to farming in Texas.[3]

Alabama went so far as to create a new class of imprisoned laborers—the county convicts, or people convicted of misdemeanors and sentenced to up to two years of hard labor. County convicts were also responsible for paying their own court costs and fees, an amount that usually totaled around fifty dollars. It was a sum that most could not afford and so they had to work off the fee at a daily rate of thirty cents in addition to their court-ordered labor sentence.[4]

In the North, prisons employed incarcerated labor in the 1820s, several decades earlier than their Southern neighbors. At first, the Northern prison system split between the penitentiary model, in which imprisoned people were expected to sit in solitary confinement to reflect on and repent their individual moral failings, and the Auburn model. The latter, named after the New York prison in which it originated, allowed imprisoned men to work together in the same room, albeit in total silence. At night, the men were returned to their solitary cells to silently reflect on their moral shortcomings.

Women were not exempt from labor. The thirty or so women who were confined in Auburn's attic were also put to work picking wool, knitting, and spooling. Unlike their male counterparts, however, silence was not enforced.[5]

In 1839, New York opened its first women's prison, the Mount Pleasant Female Prison in Ossining, after a woman became pregnant while incarcerated at Auburn.[6] Mount Pleasant also employed the Auburn model—incarcerated women worked long hours making buttons and trimming hats as well as sewing clothes for incarcerated men, but at night they were kept in their cells.[7] When superintendent Eliza Farnham attempted to make time for religious observation, educational programming, and reading, prison inspectors chastised her, arguing that the women's prison should instead focus on bringing in higher profits.[8]

Profit, both then and now, never became the motivating force behind imprisoning people. It did, however, become an attractive way for prison administrators to offset the costs of housing, clothing, feeding, and providing a modicum of care, however inadequate, to a growing number of people. In other words, prison labor derived from officials' desires to alleviate the expenses associated with the growing numbers in custody, not the other way around.

In the 1980s, as the prison population skyrocketed, the number of jobs for incarcerated people did not rise accordingly. Removing prison jobs starkly illustrated the shift from penitentiaries as sites of rehabilitation to punishment. In his 1981 photo essay on the Washington State Penitentiary, photographer John McCoy noted that jobs were scarce and that incarcerated people had few opportunities to constructively pass the time.[9]

Today the vast majority of prison jobs involve tasks that keep the prison running—sweeping the halls, working in the kitchen, and assisting with one of the few programs available. The people who perform these jobs are paid either literal pennies per hour or not at all.

While these jobs don't bring in revenue, one could argue that having incarcerated people perform these tasks for pennies, if not for free, saves the state the expense of employing people at minimum wage (as well as the costs of social security, workers' comp, and benefits). Even so, these savings are not a driving factor of mass incarceration.

If this were true, then California's notorious Pelican Bay State Prison would look very different. Pelican Bay was opened in 1989 as a dedicated super-maximum security prison (or supermax) containing the state's Security Housing Unit (SHU). Until recently, hundreds had remained in the SHU, spending years, if not decades, locked in 11-by-7-foot cells for twenty-three to twenty-four hours each day.[10] Their only physical contact came when prison officers handcuffed and escorted them out of their cells to the shower, to the indoor cage for recreation, to the law library, or to a visit behind plexiglass. None were allowed to work. The same holds true for the nearly eighty thousand people in solitary confinement across the country.

Prison jobs may be few, but they do exist—and sometimes spark headlines. Every summer, as wildfires decimate swaths of Southern California, news stories remind the general public that part of the firefighting force are California prisoners who earn one dollar a day (but whose felony convictions prohibit them from becoming professional firefighters upon release).

Other prison jobs garner less public attention but still benefit state budgets. Corcraft, a manufacturer within New York's prison system, makes metal desks, filing cabinets, tables, lockers, and storage cabinets and sells the products to government agencies, including schools, courts, police departments, and even local jails. The business also operates a call center for the state's Department of Motor Vehicles. During the coronavirus pandemic, Corcraft also began producing hand sanitizer (though its incarcerated workers were prohibited from purchasing or using it).[11] New York State's minimum wage ranges between $11.80 and $15 per hour, but Corcraft's average pay is 62 cents per hour.[12] Similar programs exist in other states, including Alabama and New Jersey. But only 6 percent of people in state prisons hold these kinds of jobs.[13] The other

94 percent either work jobs maintaining the prisons at substantially lower wages or do not work at all.

The federal prison system operates a similar program under the name UNICOR. Authorized by Congress in 1934, UNICOR provides goods and services to government contractors, such as the Department of Defense and Homeland Security, not to private sector corporations.[14] Only 13,369 (or 8 percent) of the nearly 220,000 people in federal prisons were employed in 2012.[15] As in state prisons, the other 92 percent are either relegated to in-prison jobs at substantially lower rates or do not work at all.

Immigration prisons, particularly those run by private corporations, have taken advantage of the Voluntary Work Program, in which detained immigrants are paid one dollar a day to cook meals, scrub toilets, swab floors, and do other tasks that keep the facilities running. In 2013, the New York Times estimated that at least sixty thousand of the immigrants who cycled through the nation's detention centers that year had worked for a dollar a day.[16]

Some states, like Colorado, where the minimum wage is $8.31 per hour, do allow private companies to use imprisoned laborers.[17] The women's prison in Pueblo, for instance, started a farm labor program in 2007 after anti-immigration legislation drove away regular migrant workers. Local farms pay the Department of Corrections $9.60 per hour for each imprisoned laborer, but the women earn only between $4.50 and $8 each day.[18] If a woman owes child support or restitution, the money is first applied to that balance. (When the program began, women reported keeping $4 to $5.50 per day.) The money withheld from the incarcerated women goes toward staff costs, food, and transportation. Another company, Haystack Mountain, which produces goat cheese, pays Colorado prisoners sixty-six cents a day to milk its approximately one thousand goats.[19]

At Oklahoma's Eddie Warrior Correctional Center, the state's minimum security prison for women, nearly two hundred incarcerated women work at the prison's call center contracted by private corporation ProCom. Each woman sits in a gray-blue cubicle with a computer and headset to answer incoming calls. Jenny works twelve hours on weekdays and ten hours on Saturdays transferring callers to insurance companies.[20]

Martha, on the other hand, spends her twelve-hour workdays reading from a script. Each time she answers the phone, she must chirp, "Thanks for calling the such-and-such Chrysler Chevrolet event headquarters. Congratulations! You are a winner!" before telling the caller where to go to collect their prize.[21] She has also conducted surveys about political candidates and urged callers to lobby their representatives to oppose Medicare expansion.[22] ProCom's starting pay is seventy-five cents per hour,[23] but after working eighty hours, the hourly rate rises to $1.45, the highest wage in the prison.[24]

The next highest-paying job is in the prison's saddle shop, which pays thirty-five cents per hour. Baking jobs in the prison kitchen pay $20 per month. In contrast, Oklahoma's minimum wage is $7.25 an hour.[25]

That math might also cause people to believe that prison labor is a driving force behind mass incarceration. After all, why pay workers minimum wage if a company can contract with prisons for a much lower-paid labor force?

But private companies employ only a sliver of the prison population. Any prison that markets more than ten thousand dollars' worth of goods publicly must register and be regulated by the Prison Industry Enhancement Certification Program (PIECP). The PIECP report for the first quarter of 2012 showed that only 4,675 people of the 2.3 million incarcerated at the time were employed. Those 4,675 people represented 0.25 percent of the nation's incarcerated population.[26] That number remains below 1 percent today.[27]

In addition, the prison's emphasis on security interferes with running a profit-making venture. James Kilgore, who spent six and a half years in prison, explained, "Production takes a back seat when there is violence on a yard, especially if it is directed at staff. A security situation may lock down a prison for days, weeks, or even months." When a jail or prison is locked down, all movement stops. Incarcerated people are confined to their cells or dormitories. All educational and vocational programs are canceled. "No production deadlines are going to get in the way of security," Kilgore noted.[28]

That's what happened to Martha and Jenny in September 2019 when all Oklahoma state prisons went on lockdown after fights erupted at six men's prisons. Though no fights occurred at the state's two women's prisons, they, too, were placed on lockdown. That meant that Martha and the nearly two hundred women employed at ProCom were unable to work for an entire week. The prison remained on lockdown for two more weeks, and not until the following week were Martha and forty-four other women allowed to resume work at the call center.[29]

Given those numbers, we can see that prison labor actually isn't the driving force—or even a significant force—behind mass incarceration. But, then, what is its purpose?

Prison labor makes more sense if we view it as a by-product of mass incarceration rather than as a cause. Prison labor allows some people to leave their cells and housing units for a few hours each day and earn a few dollars to pay for necessities, such as toilet paper, feminine hygiene products, or calls home—exorbitant as these items may be. At Eddie Warrior, for instance, Martha must pay $2.00 for four rolls of toilet paper, $4.65 for one ounce of laundry detergent, and $2.31 for one package of twenty-four sanitary napkins, meaning that she must work over six hours just for these basic necessities. If she wants to treat herself to a twelve-pack of Keebler fudge stripe cookies, which costs $2.26, she must work two to three hours. If she wants to call her sons or grandson, she must put money on her phone account and work more than three hours to afford each twenty-minute phone call, which costs $4.60 each.[30] Her first paycheck from the call center totaled $59.90; her second was $212.90.[31] That money not only enables her to buy necessities and treat herself to a few snacks but also allows her to save money for her dream of building on her family's land a transitional home for women released from prison.

Those are powerful incentives not to take any actions that might jeopardize her job. Martha noted that if the unit manager issued her a ticket for any misconduct, she might lose her job.[32] It's also why she and Jenny requested pseudonyms for this book.

These incentives are often overlooked by the myth of prisons as slave labor camps.[33] These sought-after and scarce prison jobs often quell the potential for inside organizing, a fact that these companies openly acknowledge. Corcraft, for instance, boasts that its jobs "help prevent disruption." In other words, people working are less likely to have the time and energy to broadly demand change.

The same holds true across the country. Despite the discrepancy between pay and profit, those who land these jobs—with their better pay and potential for more satisfaction than swabbing floors—are less likely to jeopardize them. Colorado has approximately 1,800 private-industry jobs available[34] for the nearly 20,000 people in its state prison system.[35] In New York, only 2,100 of its 51,000 prisoners can work for Corcraft. At Oklahoma's Eddie Warrior Correctional Center, the call center employs only 200 of the prison's 985 women.[36] This means that those who land slightly better paying jobs are motivated to refrain from challenging prison injustices.

Reflecting on her call center job, Martha writes, "I like it. It beats layin' in a cell."[37] Martha has been imprisoned for the past fifteen years, the latest in a series of jail and prison sentences since 1979. Not only does the pay allow her to buy necessities and a few luxury treats from the commissary, but it also lets her save money for her postprison life and mentally escape prison by talking to people who have nothing to do with her current circumstances. "I get to speak to some very nice sounding gentlemen," she wrote. "One was in Las Vegas and one was in Illinois."[38] In another letter, she reflected, "It helps keep me sane in a crazy crazy world that I live in."[39]

None of this is to say that prison labor and working conditions are not important issues. Those working inside the prisons often identify it as such and have held strikes to protest exploitative wages and other unjust conditions of prison labor. But let's be clear: prison labor—and whatever profit it might garner—is a side effect of incarceration, not a driving force.

CHAPTER 6

Race has nothing to do with mass incarceration (or, If people of color are disproportionately incarcerated, it's because they commit more crimes).

Prison is actually an outcome of a broader system of violence and harm that has its roots in slavery and colonialism.

—MARIAME KABA[1]

People of color, particularly Black and Latinx people, are more likely to be policed, criminalized, prosecuted, and incarcerated than their white counterparts. The same holds true for LGBTQ people. A person unfamiliar with US history might assume this is because members of these communities commit more crimes.

That's not true. What is true is that it's impossible to understand mass incarceration without talking about race.

Yes, Black people are disproportionately incarcerated. In 2018, approximately 32 percent of men sentenced to prison were Black, and 18 percent of sentenced women were Black.[2] By comparison, Black people (of all genders) compose only about 13.4 percent of the total US population.[3]

White people, who make up about 60.7 percent of the general population, aren't reflected in the same way inside prisons. In

2018, approximately 29 percent of all men in prison were white and 47 percent of all women sentenced were white.[4] Although the number of white women in prison nearly reflects their proportion in the outside world, the imprisonment rate for Black women (88 per 100,000 Black female residents) remains nearly double that for white women (49 per 100,000 white female residents).[5]

But, some might argue, aren't these higher numbers of Black people in handcuffs and in prison because they commit more crimes? It might appear that way until you consider the ways the legal system is structured to work against Black people at every step of the process and the historical underpinnings of both the police and the prison system as means of racialized social control.

First, let's examine the present situation. Policing practices disproportionately target Black and Latinx people. During the 1990s and early 2000s, police departments around the country used "stop and frisk" policies, in which officers stopped, questioned, and searched people they perceived as acting suspiciously. But their perceptions were profoundly rooted in racist biases of what type of person is perceived as a criminal. In 2005, the US Department of Justice found that Black and Latinx people are three times as likely as whites to be searched, arrested, threatened, or met with force when stopped by the police. Over a decade later, the same continues to be true in various cities.[6] In 2020, the continued police violence and killings of Black people led to weeks of sustained protests across all fifty US states, as well as Washington, DC; Puerto Rico; and internationally.

The probability of arrest increases if the person of color being stopped is also transgender. A 2011 study estimates that 47 percent of Black transgender people and 25 percent of Latinx transgender people can expect to be arrested at some point in their lives.[7]

Police perceptions of Black and Brown people as criminals have their roots in the country's history, particularly its criminalization of Black and indigenous people who were seen as expendable or simply undesirable during the nation's earlier days. Or, as prison abolitionist and organizer Mariame Kaba has noted, "Prison is actually an outcome of a broader system of violence and harm that has its roots in slavery and colonialism."[8]

After the abolition of slavery, former slave states passed Black Codes. As described in chapter 1, Black Codes criminalized a wide range of activities, such as being outside after a certain hour, gathering in small groups, missing work, being perceived as a vagrant, or possessing a firearm, but the laws applied only to Black people. These codes changed the color and nature of Southern imprisonment from predominantly white to predominantly Black.

But even before the Civil War, Black people were imprisoned at higher rates in the slavery-free Northern states. The first person imprisoned at the Eastern State Penitentiary, the nation's first prison, was a Black man named Charles Williams, who entered in October 1829 on a two-year sentence for burglary. Throughout the penitentiary's 150-year history, Black people were incarcerated at a higher rate than their white counterparts and also targeted in other ways. In 1844, Oregon passed a law excluding all Black settlers from the territory. Any Black settler would be punished with "not less than 20 nor more than 39 stripes" for every six months they remained.[9] Oregon passed additional laws excluding Black people from the state in 1849 and 1857. Strikingly, the last of these laws was not repealed until 1926.

Black people weren't the only racial group targeted by criminalization policies that lay the groundwork for mass incarceration. In the 1800s, California laws targeted, criminalized, and incarcerated newly displaced indigenous people for acts such as loitering and vagrancy, actions they would not have resorted to had their lands not been confiscated. The laws also allowed any nonindigenous (or white) person to make that arrest.[10] Once arrested, the indigenous person would be indentured to the highest bidder and forced to work for four months without pay.

Today Native Americans make up 1.3 percent of the country's population.[11] In prisons, however, they account for 1.4 percent of all men and 2.6 percent of all women.[12]

It's crucial to understand that the racial underpinnings of criminalization didn't end in the nineteenth century. Today we can see how racial bias plays out at every step of the criminal legal system—from policing to prosecuting to sentencing.

In 1999, the New York State attorney general found that New York police stopped and searched Black people six times more often than their white counterparts. Despite the disparity, stops of Black people were less likely to result in arrests, presumably because they were less likely to have drugs or other contraband.[13] But that didn't stop the city from enacting a stop-and-frisk policy, allowing police to stop, question, and search people. Stops climbed from 97,296 in 2002 to 313,523 in 2004. By 2010, police stops had risen to 601,285. Each year, Black people made up over half and Latinx made up approximately one-third of people stopped in New York City.[14] Advocates with the Center for Constitutional Rights filed a suit, and in 2013 a federal judge ruled that stop-and-frisk practices discriminated against Blacks and other people of color and was thus unconstitutional.[15]

Today, to counter accusations of racial bias and racial profiling, police departments are turning to predictive policing, a form of policing that relies on data, including arrests and crime, to predict future crime.

These past arrests and surveillance are frequently informed by existing police biases and past police actions, both of which adversely affect low-income Black, Brown, and immigrant communities. This means that predictive policing focuses on these same communities and, under the microscope of police surveillance, those residents are more likely to be stopped, searched, and arrested than people who live in whiter, more affluent communities, which are not constantly monitored by police. Still, predictive policing has been taken up by dozens of police forces around the

United States, leading to a disproportionate number of stops, arrests, prosecutions, and jail or prison sentences for residents in the targeted neighborhoods.

Predictive policing hasn't made neighborhoods or cities safer. Just look at Chicago where police have engaged in stop-and-frisk practices, gang policing, predictive policing, and militarized policing. Between 1972 and 1991, Chicago police detective Jon Burge participated in or approved the torture of 118 Chicagoans; under his command, men, primarily Black men, were beaten, suffocated, subjected to mock executions at gunpoint, raped with sex toys, and given electroshock to their genitals, gums, fingers, and earlobes until they confessed to whatever the police had accused them of.[16] Burge was fired in 1993, but the city's police continued to target people of color, particularly Black people, not only for arrest but for extralegal actions. Between 2004 and 2015, Chicago police detained more than seven thousand people, who had been arrested for low-level drug charges, inside a warehouse in Homan Square; they had no access to attorneys. Nearly 86 percent of those detained were Black.[17]

If these types of policing worked, notes legal scholar and author Michelle Alexander, "Chicago would be one of the safest cities in the world."[18] But the city continues to experience thousands of shootings and hundreds of murders each year—with over 530 murders in 2018 alone.[19] Instead of promoting safety, what these myriad forms of policing have done is to terrorize and lock up low-income residents of color.

This kind of predictive policing has expanded under the guise of fighting terrorism. Following the September 11, 2001, attacks on the World Trade Center, people in immigrant Muslim communities became targets of local and federal law enforcement activities. In New York, police identified "wearing traditional Islamic clothing," giving up drinking or smoking, and "becoming involved in social activism" as warning signs of radicalization.[20]

This "preventive prosecution" of possible terror suspects includes not only surveillance but also entrapment schemes in which police or informants, posing as Muslims, propose and encourage others to participate in terror attacks.[21] Though these attacks never happen, their targets are arrested, charged with terrorism-related acts, and imprisoned.

In court, it rarely matters that the conspiracy was entirely fabricated by the police agent; it may not even matter that the person never actually agreed to participate. That was what happened to Shahawar Matin Siraj, a twenty-one-year-old Pakistani American whose dominating interest was playing Pokémon. An informant befriended him under the guise of teaching him about Islam and then attempted to ensnare him in a bombing plot; Siraj said he would have to ask his mother's permission to participate. Nonetheless, police arrested Siraj. Despite the testimony of a forensic psychologist who described Siraj as having impaired critical thinking and analytical skills that left him "susceptible to the manipulations and demands of others," he was convicted and sentenced to thirty years in prison.[22] His first question upon entering prison was about access to Pokémon.[23]

Race and racism play a significant role in the courtrooms as well. Prosecutors at both the state and federal levels decide which cases to prosecute and how severe the charges will be. A study of seven hundred thousand criminal cases found that white defendants facing similar charges were far more successful in pretrial negotiations, resulting in more favorable plea bargains than Black or Latinx defendants.[24]

In 1992, federal defenders representing five Black men charged with conspiracy to distribute more than fifty grams of crack cocaine noted they had never had a white defendant charged for crack, a surprising omission given that whites make up the majority of crack offenders.[25] Suspecting that federal prosecutors were diverting white defendants to state courts, where the penalties for crack were far less severe, they filed for discovery of prosecutors' files. The government list contained more than two thousand people charged with federal crack cocaine violations over a three-year period; all but eleven were Black. None were white.[26]

Even children are not exempt from prosecutorial racism. In many states, children under age eighteen can be tried in either juvenile or adult court. Sentences meted out in juvenile court end at age twenty-one; sentences from adult court can be as harsh as life without parole. The decision on whether to charge a child as an adult or juvenile rests with the prosecutor's office and is often tinged with racism. In 2007, the Department of Justice found that, though Black youth account for only 16 percent of young people in the US, they accounted for 35 percent of youth sent to adult criminal court and 58 percent of all youth sent to adult state prison (as opposed to juvenile prisons).[27]

Ten years later, an investigation found that the district attorney of Allegheny County (the Pennsylvania county that includes Pittsburgh) charged nearly two hundred teenagers as adults in 2016 and 2017. In 85 percent of the cases, the person charged as an adult was a Black teenager between the ages of fourteen and seventeen. In contrast, Black teens between those ages make up only 20 percent of the county's total youth population.[28]

Race continues to play a significant role in mass incarceration. To ignore this fact is to ignore the underpinnings and history of policing and the modern-day prison system—and to ignore the changes necessary to dismantle the US prison system. In 2020, in recognition of this reality—coupled with the police killings of George Floyd, Breonna Taylor, and Tony McDade—sparked sustained protests in all fifty US states and internationally. In several cities, organizers followed up not by demanding the usual reforms, such as body cameras and diversity trainings, but with campaigns to defund and dismantle the police.[29]

"Don't do the crime if you can't do the time." People need to take personal responsibility for their actions.

Being in prison for years has nothing to do with causing a person to take personal responsibility for their actions.

—KNIKITA AYDELOTTE, imprisoned in Alabama

"Don't do the crime if you can't do the time." The slogan was already popular in the 1960s but became ingrained in public consciousness and morality when the 1970s TV detective show *Baretta* incorporated it into its theme song.

The slogan—and the underlying idea about taking responsibility for one's actions—has long outlived the television show. As mass incarceration has built up over the following decades, the myth of imprisonment as a method that forces people to take personal responsibility continues to inhabit the popular imagination. After all, if not prison, then what would force people to take responsibility for the harms they have caused?

The idea of individual responsibility has deep roots in American culture. It's a form of moralizing that deflects arguments about systemic injustices—such as racism, economic inequalities, misogyny, and pervasive discrimination—allowing us to focus on a person's individual shortcomings rather than challenging and eradicating larger systemic forces.

But what does personal responsibility look like? How exactly does putting someone in prison for years, if not decades, cause them to take personal responsibility?

Prisons offer few avenues for taking personal responsibility. "Being in prison for years has nothing to do with causing a person to take personal responsibility for their actions," reflected Knikita Aydelotte, who is in her eleventh year in the Alabama prison system. "There are so many women who enter the back gate at Tutwiler who did not earn a high school diploma or GED, and the state does not make them [earn one] either." But, she added, many don't sign up for GED classes while in prison; instead, she observed, "They play a lot of cards, watch a bunch of television, listen to a lot of radio, smoke, drink coffee, get high, talk on the phone, and play sex games."[1] None of these activities push a person to take responsibility for their actions or the harms that they've caused.

Jennifer Amelia Rose, a trans woman who has been in California's men's prisons for the past twenty-nine years, agrees: "Sentencing people to disproportionate time in prison only makes a person lose hope and adapt to prison life." Like Mwalimu Shakur, Rose entered prison at a relatively young—and still impressionable—age. "One becomes resigned to a life of earning status through savage acts of violence," she reflected. In the men's prisons where she has been incarcerated, those who are the most violent are usually the most respected. "When we are exposed to this type of prison culture, we cannot accept responsibility for violence."[2]

Like rehabilitative programs, programs that encourage people to address the consequences of their actions are few and the waiting lists are often long.

That doesn't mean that people in prison don't reflect on the harms they've caused—and try to make amends. In New York, John MacKenzie, serving a sentence of twenty-five years to life for fatally shooting a police officer, created a program that enabled incarcerated men to hear directly from other crime victims about the long-lasting effects of their actions. But it wasn't imprisonment that pushed MacKenzie to do so; it was his own remorse for his actions. New York state law prohibited him from reaching out to the family and loved ones of the officer he killed, so he was never able to directly express that remorse or attempt to make amends. The same prohibition holds true in other states.

In addition, for many, "doing the time" never ends. As of 2016, US prisons held 161,957 people serving life sentences.[3] Of those, 53,290 have been sentenced to life without parole, meaning that— no matter how much personal responsibility they take or how much they have changed their behavior—they will never have the opportunity to apply for parole.[4] This could act as a powerful disincentive for a person to reflect on the harms their actions have caused, let alone take responsibility for them.

Even those who are eligible to apply for parole face uphill battles proving they have taken responsibility—and feel remorse—for their actions. They frequently face parole commissioners who put more emphasis on the nature of their original crime than on any programs, counseling, and other benchmarks that they participated in during their years in prison.

That's what happened to John MacKenzie, who spent forty-one years in New York prisons, where he earned three degrees, participated in various prison programs, and, in memory of his own victim, secured ten thousand dollars in funding to create a program that allowed victims to speak directly to imprisoned men about the impact of their crimes.

None of these accomplishments mattered when he appeared before the parole board twenty-five years after entering prison in 1975. What did matter? The nature of his crime. MacKenzie appeared before the parole board ten times over a sixteen-year period. Each time, he was denied. Even after the state passed a law in 2011 requiring the parole board to consider not just the nature of the crime but also factors such as participation in rehabilitative programs, release plans, and the risk of recidivism, the parole board still denied his application. On August 3, 2016, nine days after his tenth parole denial, MacKenzie, age seventy, died by suicide.[5]

Parole denials based on the nature of the crime are so common that advocates (as well as the *New York Times*) frequently call the parole board "broken."[6] Judith Brink, an advocate with the Prison Action Network, receives hundreds of letters from New York prisoners who have been denied parole. "The majority of the people I hear from are all denied because of the nature of their crime," she said.[7] In June 2016, two months before MacKenzie's fatal parole denial, the board saw 895 applicants.[8] Only 258 (or 29 percent) were released. Despite the state's own findings that people over age sixty-five were least likely to commit new crimes, of the 33 applicants ages sixty or older, only 9 were released.[9]

At the same time, imprisonment doesn't necessarily offer healing to the person's victims or their loved ones. Parole commissioners frequently receive letters from victims and victims' families opposing the release of the person who harmed their loved one. Of course, these letters aren't representative of all victims. Those who have started to heal and move on or who are not opposed to a person's parole typically do not bother taking the time to write to the parole board. But those who do write to the board indicate that prisons have done nothing to help them heal. "Time after time, victims tell the parole board that they still feel exactly the way they did the day the crime occurred ten, fifteen, twenty years later," reflected Danielle Sered, director of the restorative justice program Common Justice. "If prison worked, survivors would feel better as a result of the incarceration of the person who hurt them. And yet so many survivors do not. Their pain continues unabated because they are relying on an intervention—incarceration—that is not equipped and was never designed to help them heal."[10]

Sered's description of what prison is *not* meant to do—"not equipped and . . . never designed to help them heal"—contradicts the idea that imprisonment encourages people to take personal responsibility for their actions. If we think of the victims, taking responsibility not only means confessing one's guilt and one's participation in harmful acts but also participating in acts to help with the victim's healing. Being locked away in a prison may mean that a person is no longer able to physically hurt a victim or their loved ones, but it also means that they are unable to make amends for the harm they caused. Instead, they are first ensnared in an adversarial legal system that encourages them to deny any wrongdoing upon penalty of lengthy imprisonment. Then they are thrust into an often hostile and violent environment that does not encourage them to take responsibility for their acts. Meanwhile, their imprisonment does nothing to ensure that victims receive counseling or other resources to help them heal from their trauma.

"We who do take advantage of the programs that prison has to offer end up growing and healing and even forgiving," wrote Sissy, who is incarcerated for fatally shooting her abusive boyfriend. "Our victims' families, however, stay stuck in a rut and remain there and never push on with their lives."[11] That's what she learned when she applied for parole. Both times, her ex-boyfriend's family voiced their opposition to the parole board, which ultimately denied her application. But Sissy will never know how much weight their opposition has had. In Alabama, the parole board, which considers nearly 210 cases each week, is not required to give a reason for denying parole, so applicants never know what they need to do to increase their chances of success the next time.[12]

There are few ways to take personal responsibility in an environment that exerts total control over movement, including when to sleep, wake, eat, and shower, and that provides little encouragement for self-reflection and personal transformation. "I'm trying to find a way to get to do community service in some way or another, so I can begin giving back to the community I offended," Aydelotte wrote. While many of the women around her pass their days in prison playing cards, watching television, reading novels, or getting high, she also notes that there are other women who would welcome the chance to do some type of service work. "But right now, there is a wall we can't get over . . . or haven't found the door to walk through."[13]

Thus, instead of encouraging people to take responsibility for the harms they've caused, prisons simply act as warehouses, removing people from society—and from any chance of trying to make amends.

PART 2

The Myths of Prisons as Service Providers and Safety Nets

CHAPTER 8

Jails and prisons provide people with needed mental health care.

If you have someone diagnosed with a mental illness,
can you think of a worse place to put them than a jail?

—TOM DART, Cook County sheriff

In 2015, a headline in *The Atlantic* screamed "America's Largest Mental Health Hospital Is a Jail."[1] The article described Chicago's Cook County Jail, the nation's fourth-largest jail system, where one in every three people has some form of mental illness.[2]

The US does not have a national healthcare system. It also does not have a national mental health care system. Access to mental health care—or lack thereof—varies from state to state and even by jurisdiction. Jail often becomes the de facto place to deposit people with mental illnesses. The National Alliance on Mental Illness estimates that two million people with mental illnesses are arrested each year.[3]

Why have jails become the de facto depository for people with mental health issues? For one, community mental health resources continue to be severely slashed. In Chicago in 2012, for instance, Mayor Rahm Emmanuel and the city council approved closing six of the city's twelve clinics; the State of Illinois closed three of its nine mental health hospitals.[4] These closures left thousands of people without access to regular mental health care and to providers with whom they could develop trust and rapport.

Cook County sheriff Tom Dart has expressed doubt that jail is the best provider for people needing mental health care, telling *The Atlantic*, "If you have someone diagnosed with a mental illness, can you think of a worse place to put them than a jail? The living units we put them in change some of that dynamic—these wide-open dormitory settings—but traditionally around the county, you find they'll be tossed in four-by-eight [foot] jail cells. I mean, can you think, if you were mentally ill, how that must feel?"[5]

In addition, the emphasis on rules and punishments works against creating an environment conducive for treating mental health. "Consider a patient who is so depressed that he does not want to leave his cell to participate in treatment or recreational programs," noted psychiatrist Terry Kupers. "If a depressed or psychotic jail prisoner remains in his single cell for a long time—isolation and inactivity that will almost certainly worsen the mental illness—officers leave him be, figuring that is best for the smooth-running of the jail."[6] But self-imposed isolation is a symptom of depression and psychosis, one that officers can easily overlook.

In contrast, in a treatment facility that is not a jail or prison, if a patient decides to stay in her room, a staff member will talk with her and try to persuade her to participate in programs. The difference is enormous. "The individual with serious mental illness who stays in his jail cell will not benefit from treatment while the patient in the community program will benefit maximally," stated Kupers.[7]

Jails and prisons often exacerbate that isolation by placing people with mental illness in solitary confinement. Solitary confinement takes various names within jails and prisons. It is sometimes called administrative or punitive segregation. In New York prisons, it's a Special Housing Unit; in California, it's a Security Housing Unit. Regardless of the name, mental health experts are increasingly in agreement that locking a person in isolation for twenty-three to twenty-four hours per day for days, weeks, months, and sometimes years is dangerous for their mental well-being.

In its 2016 report, the Public Advocacy and Treatment Center found that, in nearly 70 percent of the 230 jails surveyed, people with mental illnesses are frequently placed in solitary, which means being confined to their cell for nearly twenty-four hours each day.[8] Their only human contact comes from the officers who slide food through the slot in their cell door three times a day and from the voices of others shouting through their doors from their own isolation cells. The prolonged isolation exacerbates existing mental health disorders.

That's what happened to Monte, a young Black man with bipolar and schizoaffective disorders. When Los Angeles police arrested Monte, he had just gotten into a car accident and was in the midst of a manic episode. Though he never did anything more than yell, the officers shot him with rubber bullets and tased him before charging him with terrorism for saying something threatening to a white woman.[9]

His sister and cofounder of the Black Lives Matter movement, Patrisse Khan-Cullors, visited him in the hospital's prison wing. She recalled that his words were "unclear and slurry" except for one request: "Can I have my medication please? I don't feel well. Please?"

Two days later, he was transferred to one of the city's eight jails and placed in solitary confinement. When Khan-Cullors visited Monte there, he again asked for his medication. Despite having diagnosed him during an earlier incarceration, jail staff had only given him Advil.[10] During his incarceration, Monte was beaten, restrained to a bed, and placed in solitary confinement.

Within jails and prisons, mental health staff are frequently asked to evaluate whether being placed in solitary confinement will further erode a person's mental health. They are also asked to evaluate self-harm and suicide attempts—and to judge whether the person truly needs help or if they are faking it. But providers don't make these evaluations in a vacuum; instead, they are frequently influenced by the culture of security—and the perception that many incarcerated patients are faking their symptoms. It's a conundrum known as "dual loyalty," or a conflict between a doctor's responsibility to their patients and to their employers.

Dual loyalty can result in medical decisions and evaluations that would be extremely different outside a jail or prison setting. For instance, Candie Hailey-Means spent twenty-seven consecutive months in solitary at Rikers Island, New York's notorious island-jail complex. While in solitary, she repeatedly swallowed objects, cut herself, and hit her head against the walls. Her actions resulted in medical treatment for her injuries and mental health evaluations to determine whether she should be removed from solitary and provided with mental health treatment. But in each case, mental health staff said that her actions were manipulative and designed to get her out of isolation.

Security protocols frequently interfere with providing mental health care and often worsen preexisting conditions. In a jail, whether it's considered a mental health jail or a regular one, correctional officers are the ones in charge of the everyday minutiae. If a person breaks a rule, seems aggressive, or is assaultive, multiple officers forcefully subdue the person, usually by pepper-spraying, teargassing, or tasing them and then physically taking them down (usually by tackling) and handcuffing them. Staff then place them in isolation.

That's what happened to Ms. DM, a pregnant woman with a documented history of schizophrenia. She spent nearly three months in the mental health unit of Arizona's Maricopa County Jail, where she spent most of her days locked into her cell for twenty-three hours. At one point, she was allowed to participate in a program, but had to do so while locked away from others in a cage. Later, she refused to leave the cage, throwing crayons and paper. Though mental health staff were only feet away from her, jail officers did not ask them to help deescalate the situation; instead, the officers tased her.[11]

By contrast, in a treatment facility, Kupers notes, mental health staff "focus on seeing in advance the dissatisfaction and anger, before they mount, and assign a clinician to work 'one-on-one' with the potentially assaultive resident or patient."[12]

But the myth that jails and prisons are places where people can access mental health treatment persists, justifying and fueling the construction of "mental health units" or "mental health jails" instead of the construction of non-carceral mental health centers.

Another important point to remember—and that should be reiterated whenever jail is proposed as a mental health treatment facility—is that arrest and incarceration happen *after* a criminalized act has occurred, not before. The criminalized action may be a minor offense, usually an act of survival, such as retail theft. But in some cases, the act might lead to a fatality—sometimes the result of a prolonged lack of mental health treatment in the community.

For Marg, a mother in her early twenties living in Chicago, mental health treatment came far too late. Marg had immigrated to the United States and settled in Chicago in the 1980s. Marg already had one daughter from a previous marriage and had recently given birth to a baby boy with her second husband. One month later, her six-year-old daughter arrived to live with her.

The second birth had left Marg with postpartum depression, a condition that went undiagnosed. Unlike the shorter-term "baby blues," which includes mood swings, crying spells, anxiety, and difficulty sleeping shortly after giving birth, postpartum depression is more severe and includes withdrawing from family and friends; intense irritability and anger; feelings of hopelessness, worthlessness, shame, and guilt; severe anxiety or panic attacks; thoughts of self-harm or harm to the baby; and recurring thoughts of death or suicide. Left untreated, postpartum depression can last months, if not years.[13]

Marg was unable to access mental health, or even postpartum health services, which might have diagnosed and treated her depression with psychotherapy and/or antidepressant drugs. Instead, she was left alone—with a newborn and a six-year-old—to struggle through a rollercoaster of emotions. "I felt weak and jumpy," she recalled. "I did not sleep. I suffered depression, sadness, frequent colds, nightmares and fatigue. I was crying for no reason."[14]

Eight months later, Marg killed her six-year-old daughter. She was arrested and taken to Chicago's Cook County Jail. She was convicted of first-degree murder and sentenced to fifty-five years in prison.

Marg's story occurred in the 1990s—nearly a decade before Tom Dart took over the Cook County Jail and began changes to accommodate the need for mental health services. But even if her story had occurred more recently, a mental health jail would not have averted her daughter's death.

Had Marg had access to postpartum or mental health services in her neighborhood, a provider might have recognized her symptoms—and treated her before her condition led to tragedy. But she didn't.

Then we have to remember that the torturous conditions within jails and prisons often exacerbate—if not cause—mental health issues. The California Institution for Women (CIW), for instance, is one of three women's prisons in the state. In 2016, the prison was at 135 percent capacity, housing 1,886 women in a facility designed for 1,398. People inside the prison describe high levels of drug use and mental health problems. Between 2013 and 2015, the prison had sixty-five suicide attempts and five successful suicides—a rate that is five times more than all of the state's other prisons and eight times the rate for women's prisons nationwide. Lindsay Hayes, a national suicide prevention expert, audited the prison in 2013 and again in 2015; in his 2016 report, he noted that CIW continued to exhibit poor suicide prevention practices.[15]

Jenny, who remains incarcerated at CIW, blames the over-crowding for what she calls "an extreme increase in the internal drug trade in the prison system and all the associated fights, lock-downs and increased restrictions." Reflecting on the twelve sui-cide attempts in October 2015 alone,[16] she wrote, "The internal drug trade is alive and well and no one seems to be able to stop it. That is, in my opinion, where most of the suicide attempts come from—unpaid drug debts, hopelessness and oppression."[17]

Amber, who also remains imprisoned, remembers that hope-lessness very well. While incarcerated at CIW, she saw mental health staff every ninety days for five-minute appointments. That wasn't enough, and, she recalled, "As time went on and I became more and more frustrated by the lack of anything to take my mind off my emptiness, I got more lonely and hopeless."

Amber stopped talking to her friends, stopped eating, lost in-terest in her appearance, and began losing weight. She told men-tal health staff that she wanted to stop taking medication. No one questioned her decision. Then she and another woman made a joint suicide pact. Amber felt a rush of relief after making that decision. "I was happy. I knew my misery and pain were ending," she re-called. "This seemed to be the only way." The two slit their throats, losing consciousness. But someone found them and alerted staff, who rushed them to the hospital.

Once returned to the prison, both women were placed on sui-cide watch. Amber described suicide watch as a place "where they strip you naked and put a hard gown on you, basically a life jacket. They give you a blanket made of the same material and have a bright light on with a nurse watching and recording [on paper] your every move. . . . You are not allowed anything for the first week. Then you can 'earn' a book. And maybe a muumuu gown if you are calm and cooperative. You aren't even allowed a roll of toilet paper. When you need to use the toilet [in your cell], they hand you a tiny bit and watch you use it." Amber spent two weeks under these conditions before being moved to the prison's specialty care unit. She described the programming as fourteen hours a week of coloring, watching movies, singing karaoke, and walking.[18]

As with nearly every other aspect of incarceration, race plays a significant role in a person's access to mental health care. Homer Venters, the former chief medical officer for New York City Correctional Health Services, analyzed first-time admissions to the city's jails between 2011 and 2013. He examined access to mental health services and placement in solitary confinement for the 45,189 people entering jail for the first time. Of those 45,189 people, 46 percent were Black, 41 percent Latinx, 9 percent white, and 4 percent were identified as "other."

Despite making up the majority of new jail admissions, Black and Latinx people were less likely to receive mental health treatment. Only half as many Black and Latinx people accessed the jail's mental health services compared to their white counterparts. However, Black people were 2.52 times more likely than whites to be placed in solitary; Latinx people were 1.88 times more likely than whites.[19]

The banality and brutality of mental health treatment behind bars has aftereffects even after a person is released, often discouraging them from seeking care in the community. Khan-Cullors recalled that, after her brother Monte was released from prison, he stopped taking his medications. He suffered another manic episode and destroyed his ex-girlfriend's apartment. A 911 call would have brought police along with an ambulance, and, given that Monte's every police interaction had resulted in his being beaten and arrested, Khan-Cullors and her family decided instead to try persuading Monte to voluntarily go to the hospital. But, after years of incarceration, Monte associated mental health care with violence, restraints, and little or no actual treatment.

His family persisted in reasoning, cajoling, and arguing, and eventually Monte agreed. They drove him to the hospital, and he was brought in as a patient with dignity and rights, not as a Black man in handcuffs.

If jails and prisons aren't purveyors of mental health care for society's most underresourced, then what is the solution?

"This is a question of what we [as a society] invest in," Khan-Cullors said. "We have invested billions of dollars into police and incarceration and very little funds into preventing and intervening in crises."[20]

CHAPTER 9

People in prison "jump the line" for life-saving medical care.

Before she can even get on the bus to go to an outside medical provider, she is strip-searched, handcuffed, shackled at her waist and feet, and brought to the prison's back gate where she is strip-searched again. "You remain in restraints throughout the trip," Kamadia described, even if the trip lasts six to seven hours.

"PRISONER GETS $1M HEART TRANSPLANT."
"N.C. MAN ALLEGEDLY ROBS BANK OF $1 TO GET HEALTH CARE IN JAIL."
"DEATH-ROW INMATE SEEKS ORGAN TRANSPLANT."[1]

Reading these headlines might lead one to conclude that people in prison "jump the line" for life-saving medical care while law-abiding people languish—and sometimes die—waiting for that same care on the outside.

That's not true.

What is true is that in a country without universal healthcare, people behind bars are the only ones with a constitutional right to medical care. In its 1976 *Estelle v. Gamble* decision, the Supreme Court ruled that deliberate indifference to an incarcerated person's serious medical needs violates the Eighth Amendment, which prohibits cruel and unusual punishment. In theory, jails and prisons have a constitutional obligation to provide medical care to the people in custody.

What that means in practice, however, is very different. The Supreme Court decision did not specify the quality of care that jails and prisons must provide to patients in custody; it simply mandated that they do so.

The right to healthcare clashes with the overriding concern in any jail or prison: security. This focus means that security staff, not medical providers, are often the first ones to make decisions about whether the person can leave their cell or housing unit to seek medical attention.

For instance, at Rikers Island each of the eight jail buildings has its own medical clinic. But that doesn't mean if a person feels sick or needs care, they can readily access it. First, the sick person must tell the officer on the housing unit. Then it's up to the officer to submit that person's healthcare requests to medical staff, but, according to jail medical staff, they don't always do so.

In 2013, jail officials at Rikers further impeded access to healthcare when they stopped allowing incarcerated patients to walk to the clinics alone; instead, a guard was required to escort people to the clinic. The result? People missed their appointments nearly half the time. This wasn't because of animosity from jail officers, but simply because it was too much hassle to escort every individual to the clinic.[2]

In response, medical providers gave jail staff lists of must-see patients whom they feared might die without receiving care. But these improvements were often short-lived, ending when a sympathetic official was promoted, transferred, or fired. At that point, noted Homer Venters, the former chief medical officer for the city's jails, "We would fall back to half or fewer of our patients being produced [for medical visits]."[3]

In 2020, as COVID-19 exploded into a global health crisis, this lack of medical care—coupled with conditions that made it impossible to follow CDC recommendations of social distancing and frequent handwashing—quickly brought the island-jail complex to a crisis point. Even as advocates and attorneys pushed city officials and judges to decrease the population by nearly 1,500, the infection rate soared from 1.5 percent (or 75 cases among 5,169 people) in late March to 9.8 percent (or 376 among 3,836 people) on May 1.[4] Even during the pandemic, staff prevented people from accessing medical care—sometimes brutally. In at least one instance, jail guards pepper-sprayed eight people who tried to go to the jail clinic after the person handling their food displayed flu-like symptoms and was removed from their unit.[5]

Sometimes staff delays in calling for medical attention can be deadly. In 2014, one year after Rikers began requiring officers to escort people to medical care, forty-six-year-old Carlos Mercado fell into a diabetic coma and died fifteen hours after entering the jail. He had requested medical treatment from both jail and medical staff but to no avail.[6] Jail surveillance video showed Mercado walking unsteadily holding a plastic bag full of his own vomit. When he collapsed onto the floor, he was left there for three minutes while corrections officers stepped over him.[7]

Staff gatekeeping to medical care—and its deadly consequences—aren't limited to New York City. In 2017, staff at Washington's Snohomish County Jail ignored thirty-four-year-old Piper Travis as her health deteriorated during her two weeks in custody. One week after arriving at the jail, a deputy found her crying on the floor from what she said was a bad headache and an "uncommon level of pain." In response, the jail nurse gave her an ibuprofen but made no plans for follow-up care. In the ensuing days, Travis struggled to respond to directions, talked incoherently, and soiled herself. Jail employees reportedly suggested that Travis was faking her symptoms; one deputy even suggested placing her in solitary, writing, "MAX is a good place for her." When jail staff finally called medical providers, Travis had a temperature of 102 degrees; she was hyperventilating, foaming at the mouth, and had seizure-like symptoms. She died four days later in the hospital of meningitis, sepsis, and acute respiratory distress.[8] Three years earlier, jail staff had openly taunted another woman in custody as she suffered nine days of heroin withdrawal; she died of a heart attack while in custody.[9]

Jails and prisons are not equipped to provide specialized medical care. If such care is needed, medical staff may recommend that the patient be taken to an outside clinic or hospital. If that recommendation is approved—and it often is not—two officers must escort the patient at all times. The person is not only handcuffed but fully shackled, meaning their handcuffs are tethered to a chain around their waist. They are also cuffed in leg irons, which are tethered to their waist by another chain.

That's why Kamadia doesn't seek off-site medical care. Before she can even get on the bus to go to an outside medical provider, she is strip-searched, handcuffed, shackled at her waist and feet, and brought to the prison's back gate where she is strip-searched again. "You remain in restraints throughout the trip," she described, even if the trip lasts six to seven hours. Because Kamadia is in solitary confinement, she is separated from others on the bus. The toilet is about a foot away from her, "usually overflowing, the smell is putrid." If she needs to use it, she must struggle, with the full restraints on, not only to lift the toilet seat but also to remove her pants and panties. (Those not in solitary can enlist another person to help them remove their pants and underwear and stand in front of them to ensure a modicum of privacy.) In addition, the bus has no toilet paper. "Many girls don't drink or eat, so they don't have to use the restroom," she said. Kamadia, now in her late forties, hasn't sought medical care for three years.[10]

Then there's the financial hurdle to medical care. Forty-two states (as well as the federal prison system) require a co-pay from incarcerated patients. These co-pays range from three to five dollars, though some can be as high as $7.50 per visit.[11] This may seem like peanuts, especially compared to the co-pays required for people outside of prison, but incarcerated people earn only pennies an hour at their prison jobs. Given that there are not enough positions for the hundreds, if not thousands, of people incarcerated in each state, many do not have prison jobs at all. Thus, even these few dollars can place healthcare out of reach for those in prison.[12]

In addition, some states, such as Alabama, Arkansas, Florida, Georgia, Mississippi, South Carolina, and Texas, pay incarcerated people nothing for their work but still charge them co-pays for medical care.[13] In 2011, Texas legislators changed the state's prison co-pay system to a flat yearly fee of one hundred dollars.[14] But imprisoned people can avoid that extravagant price tag by eschewing medical care—and it seems they do: in 2014, three years after the co-pay system changed, only 15,000 of the nearly 150,000 incarcerated Texans paid the one-hundred-dollar healthcare fee.[15]

Nearly half of state prison systems and many local jails contract with private for-profit corporations to provide medical care. This means a private company receives a contract for a certain sum of money to provide healthcare to incarcerated patients. To ensure the maximum amount of profits, these corporations shave expenses by hiring fewer (and often less-qualified and less-paid) staff members, requiring long and arduous processes for expensive medical care, and withholding treatment altogether.

Michigan's prisons, for instance, have a five-year $715.7 million contract with the private company Corizon to provide medical and mental health care to people in custody. More than half of its prisoners (51.6 percent) are on at least one medication.[16] But in the two and a half years since Michigan hired Corizon, the state has withheld $1.6 million in payments to the corporation for violating their contract regarding the timeliness of care in routine and chronic care appointments.

Prison healthcare systems, whether privatized or state run, have a hard time attracting and retaining qualified health professionals. But private healthcare providers often pay medical and mental health professionals less than state prisons—and don't offer the same benefits. For instance, Corizon's hourly pay for a registered nurse is $30, or $62,000 per year.[17] In contrast, the average hourly pay for a registered nurse working for the California

Department of Corrections and Rehabilitation is $51, or $107,000 per year.[18]

Healthcare makes up 16 percent of the budget for the Michigan Department of Corrections, but in February 2019 Michigan's prison system still had eighty-six vacant nurse positions and forty-four vacant licensed practical nurse positions.[19] With so many job vacancies across a system of 38,678 incarcerated people, Corizon cannot provide round-the-clock nursing or medical care.[20]

The quality of Corizon's care for incarcerated patients has repeatedly come under fire. In New York City, Corizon held the contract to provide jail medical care until 2015. The company has been sued by over two dozen New Yorkers, including the family of Carlos Mercado, over the course of two years.

The negative publicity, lawsuits, and hefty settlements have not deterred local jails and state prisons from using private healthcare corporations. As of February 2019, Corizon had contracts to provide healthcare to 301 jails and prisons in 22 states.[21] One of its main competitors, Wexford, boasts that it provides healthcare for 120 correctional institutions in 13 states.[22] Another competitor, Wellpath (formerly Correct Care Solutions), boasts contracts in 550 jails, prisons, and behavioral health facilities across the United States and Australia.[23]

Regardless of whether healthcare is privatized, medical staff must grapple with dual loyalty—to the patient and to the prison system—a conundrum in which all interactions with patients are influenced by the extreme security setting. The effects of dual loyalty might sometimes be so slight as to be barely noticeable—by the medical provider. Venters explained, "Most of the time, dual loyalty exerts a mild influence that we might not notice, such as rethinking writing an order for an asthma inhaler (which requires front- instead of rear-cuffing) or for a cane (which could be used as a weapon)."[24]

Dual loyalty can be more extreme, preventing medical staff from recognizing and recommending urgent medical care. Venters recounted one instance in which correctional officers caused a man at the jail to fracture his hip. The jail nurse examined him and ordered that he be taken to the hospital. But security staff insisted the patient was faking his symptoms. The doctor sided with the security staff. In the medical record that documented his physical examination, the doctor wrote, a "textbook description of a fracture: limb shortening and rotation." In his assessment, however, the doctor ignored his own description, writing that there was unclear evidence of a hip fracture and that instead of being brought to the hospital in an ambulance, the man should be driven by van to the jail's X-ray facility.[25]

Dual loyalty plays out in jails and prisons across the country, resulting in some patients being denied urgently needed medical care.

This confluence of factors—staff indifference, medical understaffing, and dual loyalty—can become deadly. In 2013, Venters and his medical team began tracking "jail attributable" deaths, or deaths in which the systemic or individual errors in the jail system played a significant role in a person's death. These deaths resulted from officers refusing to call for medical help or refusing to escort people to the medical unit, violence inflicted by jail staff, and a lack of treatment for preexisting or acute conditions.

Jail attributable deaths represent 10 to 20 percent of all deaths in New York City's jails each year. No other correctional healthcare system or oversight body (such as the US Department of Justice) uses the term "jail attributable death," so there is no way to quantify nationally how often jails (and prisons) contribute to the death of people in custody.[26]

Then there's the issue of cost. State officials, balancing budgets already stretched thin by the ballooning costs of incarcerating thousands of people, balk at spending money on costly treatment.

That's been the case for hepatitis C treatment. In 2019, the Infectious Diseases Society of America estimated that 30 percent of all people living with hepatitis C spend at least part of the year in a correctional institution—a much higher rate than the 1 percent outside of prison.[27] These numbers have repercussions for people on the outside as well. In 1996, approximately 1.4 million people released from jails or prisons had hepatitis C, making up 31 percent of the 4.5 million people with the virus nationwide at that time.[28]

But treatment for hepatitis C, whether in prison or outside, is expensive. In 2013, the Food and Drug Administration approved drugs that shorten treatment to twelve weeks and eliminate side effects caused by other treatments; the new drugs have a 90 percent success rate.[29] Still, the cheapest price for a course of treatment is $26,400, a cost that already-strained prison budgets are often not eager to incur.[30]

Massachusetts, for instance, spends an average of $55,170 per prisoner each year.[31] In 2015, that totaled more than $596 million for the 10,813 people in the state's prisons.[32] That same year, more than 1,500 people in the state's prisons had hepatitis C. Treating all 1,500-plus incarcerated patients would have cost another $40 million. Thus, only three received treatment.[33]

That led two men to file a class-action lawsuit against the state's Department of Correction for withholding hepatitis treatment. Three years later, in 2018, the department agreed to a settlement that overhauls its protocol for identifying, assessing, and treating people with hepatitis.[34]

The myth that incarcerated people "jump the line" for life-saving medical care disguises the realities of healthcare behind bars and diverts the conversation from shifting the resources from incarceration to outside communities. The COVID-19 pandemic behind bars is a stark illustration of the failure of jails and prisons to provide even basic care. As of May 21, 2021, there have been over 397,000 confirmed cases and 2,680 deaths among incarcerated people in the United States. Among staff, there have been nearly 27,000 confirmed cases and 75 deaths.[35]

Incarcerating people, noted Joel Thompson, a staff attorney with Prisoners' Legal Services of Massachusetts and co-counsel on the hepatitis class-action lawsuit, is "a choice that we as a society make. . . . If you want to incarcerate people [at] the rate that we do and for the duration that we currently do, you need to confront the costs. If you don't like that cost, figure out a different criminal justice policy, so you can apply those resources somewhere else."[36]

CHAPTER 10

Incarceration is an effective way to get people into drug treatment.

Not one day that I spent in jail helped me work through my addiction.

—MAGGIE LUNA

Maggie Luna, a Texas mother of three, struggled with a heroin addiction for twenty years. Her addiction led to arrests; those arrests led to multiple jail and prison stints.[1] "Not one day that I spent in jail helped me work through my addiction," she reflected.

When Luna was arrested for writing bad checks, the investigator told her that if she cooperated, she'd ensure that Luna didn't get jail time. Luna was eager to return home to her children—a three-week-old, a one-year-old, and a three-year-old—and admitted to everything. But rather than being allowed to go home, she was indicted with a bond of fifty thousand dollars.

Luna did not have fifty thousand dollars. If she had, she would not have had to write bad checks to fund her addiction. Or perhaps she would have checked herself into a private drug treatment center. Luna scrambled to find someone to care for her three children to keep them from vanishing into the child welfare and foster care system. Fortunately, the father of her three-year-old offered to care not only for their child but for the other siblings as well. Luna was sentenced to two years in state prison. She was released fourteen months later with no job prospects, no new skills, no money, and a felony record, which made it impossible for her to find a job that paid for adequate housing. She found an apartment where she and her children shared one bed. Someone noticed the family's sleeping arrangements and called child welfare officials, who removed her children.

Luna ultimately lost custody of her children, a devastation that sent her spiraling into the abyss of addiction. She was arrested again, this time for drug possession, and sentenced to one year in state jail. (In Texas, people sentenced to less than two years serve their time in state jails, which are run by the Texas Department of Criminal Justice. These differ from the county jails, where people are held while awaiting trial. Texas state prisons hold people sentenced to more than two years of confinement.)

In the state jail, Luna was placed in the drug treatment program. But the treatment was dehumanizing and did not help her address the underlying issues fueling her addiction. Released one year later, she recalled, "I came out like a caged animal."

Luna finally found a community-based residential treatment program. It also provided transitional housing, enabling her to live in a safe and supportive environment as she navigated recovery. She has now been sober for two years.

Luna's story is not an exception. In a Texas prison, Kamadia recently said good-bye to her friend Brenda, who was walking out of prison for the fourteenth time. Though each of Brenda's fourteen prison sentences were related to her addiction, she was never offered drug treatment. Instead, Brenda attempted to treat herself by immersing herself in scripture. "The last time I saw her, she was making parole," Kamadia recalled. "She said to me, 'I prayed for God not to let me out unless he's sure I'll remain clean.'" But Brenda's parole will stretch for the rest of her life and, with no treatment, counseling, or strategy aside from scripture, the chances that Brenda will relapse and end up back in prison remain high.[2]

It's not just Texas where incarceration replaces drug treatment for the poor. In liberal California, Susan Burton was pushed through a revolving door of addiction, arrest, and imprisonment for fifteen years. "Jail had done nothing to stop my addiction," she wrote.[3] None of the programs addressed the fact that her addiction was rooted in a childhood history of abuse followed by the hit-and-run death of her five-year-old son by a police officer. (The officer was never charged.)

Instead of addressing underlying traumas, prison inflicts it as an everyday practice. Burton explained:

> Guards might come into your living area and have you strip buck-naked. Or they might take all of your property and destroy it and call it a locker search. And if you say anything, you would be beat or put into the lock-up or what we call the Hole. You're walking on pins and needles being careful not to get the wrath of the prison punishment. They did not address trauma. There was nothing for it. Sometimes some of the women would create something [a program or group], but the prison didn't do that.[4]

Prison practices frequently replicate past experiences of trauma and violence, which are often underlying causes of substance abuse. At the same time, the overmedication prevalent in prisons across the country ensures that people can continue to self-medicate and abuse substances. In Texas, Kamadia noted that incarcerated women who are indigent (meaning they do not have family or loved ones who send them money) will go to mental health services and request to be put on psychotropic medications. They then sell their medications to others in exchange for commissary or hygiene items. Thus, Kamadia noted, women with addiction issues simply "replace one addiction with another. The girl who was on heroin is now purchasing Tegretols—crushing and snorting them."[5]

Then there's the question of whether a person is even able to get into a prison treatment program.

In March 2019, the director of the Arizona prison system's Inmate Programs and Reentry told the state's House Judiciary Committee, "I could not today treat everyone in the system who needed treatment immediately," she said. "The need of the inmates is greater than our capacity to deliver."[6] According to Bill Lamoreaux, the public information officer for the Department of Corrections, the Arizona prison system has a hard time recruiting qualified substance abuse counselors.[7] Only three thousand of the state's forty-two thousand incarcerated people are able to access drug treatment programs within the prison system.[8]

At the same time, prisons penalize those who continue to use substances. That same month that its administrators admitted their inability to provide drug treatment, the Arizona Department of Corrections enacted a new policy in which people who overdose and need to be taken to the hospital will be charged for all medical-related expenses and staff overtime.[9]

If jails and prisons aren't an effective way to get people into drug treatment, what is? For that, we should look at Susan Burton's experience. After fifteen years of the revolving door between jail, prison, and the streets, her brother paid for her to enter a private treatment facility in Santa Monica, California. Only then was Burton able to address the underlying causes of her addiction, including pervasive childhood violence and abuse as well as the death of her son. In addition, the contrast between the private program and the prison programs to which she had previously been relegated to opened her eyes about the root causes of her own addiction and what was needed to address them.

I saw a whole different world, a whole different approach to what was happening in South L.A. They're not criminalized in the beach city. They were treated with resources, with solutions like going to a treatment facility, getting a paper to go to 12-step meetings and bringing that back to the judge. But they weren't put in chains, they weren't thrown into cages, they weren't criminalized. . . .

It was a safe place and I was treated kindly. . . . I don't think I had been treated that way in my lifetime, and I was 46 years old. It was a place that allowed me to access weekly therapy sessions that made a huge difference in opening up the past trauma and addressing it in a safe environment with a skilled person. That put me on the road to healing. The 12 Steps of Alcoholics Anonymous allowed me, with that healing, to not be resentful or angry, but have a way to resolve the issues and experiences that I had had. I used all those tools and I became stronger. I became more useful to myself and to the world. I became a warrior.[10]

The myth that jails and prisons are effective avenues to get people into drug treatment has been used to justify the continued arrests and imprisonment of drug users. Like the myths of prisons as providers of mental health and medical care, this myth diverts attention and resources from the question of why such treatment, particularly quality treatment, remains out of reach for so many in society.

PART 3

The Invisible People
Behind the Walls

CHAPTER 11

Mass incarceration only affects Black cisgender men.

No data is kept on the number of trans women en-snared in the criminal legal system. We don't know how many are in prison; we also don't know how often they're barred from accessing non-prison alternatives.

M ass incarceration is often framed as a men's issue, most fre-quently as a Black men's issue. But focusing primarily on men ignores the fact that, since 1980, women's incarceration has grown at twice the rate of men's.[1] Attention to women behind bars has failed to increase at the same pace. Instead, prison issues continue to be framed—and told—as men's issues. Men are the people who are incarcerated; women, when they are mentioned, are their loved ones and supporters—wives, girlfriends, mothers, and daughters.

Part of the reason for their frequent omission is that the num-ber of women behind bars is still relatively small compared to the male prison population. For instance, in 2018 women made up 7.6 percent of the country's prison population, or people who had been convicted and sentenced to state or federal prison, and 15 percent of the nation's jail population.[2] (About 115,100 were confined in women's jails. Another 104,200 were in state or fed-eral women's prisons.)[3]

Also lost in this narrative is the fact that lesbian, gay, and bi-sexual people are disproportionately incarcerated. A 2017 analysis found that while lesbians, gay men, and bisexuals make up approximately 3.5 percent of the US population, their numbers are higher in prison: 5.5 percent of men in prison are gay or bisexual, and 33.3 percent of women in prison are lesbian or bisexual.[4]

The framing of mass incarceration as a Black men's issue also overlooks the numbers of trans women behind bars. In nearly every state, trans people are classified according to the sex assigned to them at birth and sent to the corresponding prison. That means that the vast majority of trans women are incarcerated in men's jails, prisons, and immigrant detention centers. Similarly, trans men are held in women's jails, prisons, and immigrant detention centers. In rare instances, usually after experiencing prolonged sexual and physical violence in a men's prison followed by a protracted legal fight, a trans woman is transferred to a women's prison.[5]

No government agency tracks the number of incarcerated transgender, intersex, or gender-variant people across the nation—or even in a given state. The Department of Justice estimated that, between 2011 and 2012, there were 3,209 trans people in state and federal prisons and another 1,709 in local jails.[6] That is the most recent national statistic available.[7]

The high rate of incarceration, especially compared to the number of trans people in the overall US population, is the result of racist and transphobic policing and widespread (and often legalized) discrimination that keeps many trans people in poverty.

For many trans women of color, their mere existence is a reason for police to stop, question, and arrest them. That's what happened to Bianey García. In 2008, she and her boyfriend were walking down the street when NYPD officers stopped her. They pushed her to the ground, searched her purse, and found condoms. Citing those condoms as evidence of prostitution, they arrested her. When her boyfriend intervened, explaining that he was her boyfriend, they threatened him with arrest as well.

After a few hours, García was released. But the experience—and subsequent fear of being arrested simply for existing—remained. "The police act like we are nothing," she reflected.[8]

Her experience is not an anomaly. A 2011 study estimated that 47 percent of Black transgender people, 30 percent of Native American transgender people, 25 percent of Latinx transgender people, 13 percent of Asian transgender people, and 12 percent of white transgender people can expect to be arrested at some point in their lives.[9]

There aren't similar statistics breaking down the likelihood of arrest by race, but we do know in that same year, Black people accounted for 28 percent (or 2.9 million arrests) of the 10.35 million arrests in the United States, and white people accounted for 69 percent (or 7.1 million arrests). The FBI does not track arrests of Latinx people separately.[10]

Keep in mind that, according to the 2010 census, Black people accounted for only 12.6 percent of the US population; Latinx people accounted for 16.3 percent; and white people, 72.4 percent.[11] So regardless of gender or gender identity, Black people are more likely to be arrested than their white counterparts. But when factoring in gender identity—and police stereotypes and biases against trans women, particularly trans women of color—the incidence of arrest is greater. As García's experience illustrates, police often profile trans women of color as sex workers, a phenomenon so common that it's been dubbed "walking while trans."[12]

Trans women's disproportionate number of arrests also stem from poverty—and the lack of legal protections that push and often keep trans people in poverty. In 2016, North Carolina made headlines when state lawmakers passed a bill banning trans people from using public bathrooms in accordance with their gender identity. That year, lawmakers in sixteen other states introduced more than forty anti-trans bills in efforts to codify the exclusion of trans people from legal protections.

The lack of legal protections extends to employment discrimination, thus increasing the risk of poverty. On June 15, 2020, the US Supreme Court ruled that the 1964 Civil Rights Act, which prohibits workplace discrimination based on sex, extends to LGBTQ people. At least half of the fifty US states had previously allowed employers to fire workers for being gay or trans.[13] A study by the National Center for Transgender Equality found that more than one in four trans people had lost a job due to bias. More than three-quarters have experienced some form of workplace discrimination, such as not being hired and, if they are hired, privacy violations, harassment, and even violence. Many have reported changing jobs to avoid discrimination. This widespread discrimination and lack of protection often result in fewer job opportunities, lower wages, and higher rates of poverty for trans people. A 2016 study found that 15 percent of trans respondents earn less than ten thousand dollars per year, compared to 4 percent of the general population.[14]

———

Even when there are legal protections for trans people, they often fall short. Twenty-three states already had clear laws or policies prohibiting workplace discrimination against trans people, but such policies are not always put into practice. In 2002, for instance, the New York City Council passed the Transgender Rights Bill to expand gender-based protections and to make explicit that the law prohibits discrimination against people based on gender identity.[15]

Five years later, a 2007 study found that trans and gender-nonconforming people suffer pervasive discrimination in—and therefore diminished access to—housing, employment, healthcare, education, public benefits, and social services.[16] This lack of access pushes a disproportionate number of transgender youths and adults into criminalized means of survival, such as sex work, drug sales, or theft. The study also found that, because of entrenched social stigma, transgender people encounter pervasive violence and physical brutality from family members, community members, and the police. Discrimination and violence often prevent transgender people from accessing shelters, foster care, Medicaid, public entitlements, and social safety nets, which would enable them to survive without turning to illegal activities. As a result, transgender people are disproportionately poor, homeless, criminalized, and imprisoned.

New York City is not the only place where codified protections have failed to translate into actual protections. In San Francisco, which has had antidiscrimination laws since 1994, the Department of Public Health found that more than 30 percent of trans women had been incarcerated during the preceding twelve months.[17] The State of California has prohibited employment discrimination against trans people since 2004. But trans people in California are still twice as likely to fall below the federal poverty line than the general population, with as many as one in five people reporting homelessness since first identifying as transgender.

In Georgia, only three counties prohibit discrimination against trans people in public employment.[18] Athens-Clarke County is one of them. But when Ashley Diamond, a young Black trans woman, moved to town, she found that if she was open about her gender identity, employers would not hire her. If she hid her identity and employers later found out, she was fired.

To survive, Diamond turned to criminalized acts, such as fishing Taco Bell receipts from the trash to get refunds, breaking into her best friend's apartment and stealing checks, and violating probation. Those acts led to arrests, with the last charge landing her in a men's prison on a twelve-year sentence. According to the *New York Times*, the sentencing judge in her hometown of Rome, which lacks antidiscrimination laws, told her, "Hopefully, you'll get all this behind you. When you do, you probably just need to go somewhere where you can get a job and not have to steal and shoplift and forge things to survive. You might be better off if you lived somewhere that was more accepting to the way that you live."[19] She was sent to men's prisons, where she endured repeated physical and sexual assaults by the men around her.

Diamond's horrifying experience is not unusual. When trans people are incarcerated, they are typically sent to jails and prisons that match the sex assigned to them at birth. This means that trans men are housed in women's facilities while the vast majority of trans women are confined in male facilities. For the latter, such placement puts them at dangerously high risks for sexual assault. One study found that 59 percent of trans women in California's men's prisons had been sexually assaulted while incarcerated, compared to 4 percent of the cisgender male population.[20] Trans women in men's prisons also experience physical and verbal harassment and abuse by both prison staff and other incarcerated men.

That's what happened to Strawberry Hampton, a Black trans woman incarcerated in Illinois, where people are imprisoned according to their genitalia. Hampton spent three and a half years in the state's male prisons. There she was sexually harassed and abused by staff members. When she threatened to file a complaint, sixteen staff members brutally beat her. When Hampton filed the complaint the next day, prison staff placed her in solitary confinement, where they continued to sexually harass and physically abuse her. They also placed her in a cell with a man known to be aggressive, then watched as the man beat Hampton.[21]

Hampton sued the prison system for the right to be housed in a women's prison. In December 2018, the Illinois Department of Corrections settled the lawsuit, agreeing to transfer her to one of the state's two women's prisons. Four months later, it settled a similar lawsuit with twenty-nine-year-old Janiah Monroe, who endured physical and sexual abuse in men's prisons for over a decade. In April 2019, Monroe was also moved to a women's prison.[22]

Despite these victories and their precedents for other incarcerated trans women, it's important to note that the majority of trans women continue to be held in men's prisons. Even if they are moved to women's prisons, they continue to face substandard medical and mental health care as well as dehumanizing and alienating conditions.

If a judge is willing to consider an alternative to incarceration, few programs are willing to recognize and respect trans people's gender identity. In 2008, Sabire Wilson, a transgender woman who was arrested for drug possession, accepted a plea bargain allowing her to go to a drug treatment center instead of prison. She chose a treatment center that purported to be gay- and lesbian-friendly. However, because Wilson's assigned sex at birth was male, the admissions counselor agreed to admit her only if she used the male dormitories and bathroom. Wilson agreed so long as staff allowed her to dress and present as a woman.

The following year, a senior counselor invited Wilson to participate in a new group for women "where clients could discuss gender issues associated with addiction." When two or three women complained about her participation, the director allegedly told her that the counselor should have put her in a male group instead. Although Wilson had excelled in the center's career training program, had been made a "resident structure senior coordinator," and had been lauded as "a valued member" who had "earned the respect of the community" by thirty-eight men and women on her unit, the director told Wilson that the district attorney would discharge her to the court, which meant she faced incarceration if she didn't find another treatment program.[23] Wilson said that participating in the new treatment program led to severe depression, low self-esteem, paranoia, and a drug relapse, which ultimately led to another arrest and a thirty-month sentence in a supermax men's prison. There, she was held in isolation for nearly twenty-four hours a day.

No data is kept on the number of trans women ensnared in the criminal legal system, so just as we don't know how many are in prison, we also don't know how often they're barred from accessing nonprison alternatives.

The myth that mass incarceration is a men's issue conceals the existence of trans and gender-nonconforming people behind bars—as well as the social, political, and economic realities that push them into prison. So long as their existence—and issues—remain invisible, few changes will be made to address the policies that criminalize and incarcerate them.

"People should get involved in changing policies that keep people in prisons, like exclusion from employment, housing, public assistance," wrote CeCe McDonald, a Black trans woman who spent nineteen months in a Minnesota men's prison after defending herself from a violent homophobic attack on the street. "These are just a few things that will keep people out of prisons and lead to the dismantling of these facilities."[24]

CHAPTER 12

Bringing up a history of abuse and violence is simply an "abuse excuse."

*At least 60 percent of people in women's prisons
have a history of physical or sexual abuse; in
some prisons, the rate is as high as 94 percent.*[1]

Enter any women's prison and you'll find that the majority of the
people confined have a history of abuse and violence inflicted
upon them, even before they were arrested. For countless women,
that history of abuse and violence propelled them onto a pathway to
prison—a phenomenon so common that advocates have dubbed it
the "abuse-to-prison pipeline."[2]

"Story after story after story can be heard in Mabel Bassett,"
wrote Mary Fish in a letter from the Mabel Bassett Correctional
Center, Oklahoma's largest women's prison. For years, Oklahoma
has had the dubious distinction of having the nation's highest female incarceration rate. Since 1997, the state has also had one of
the country's highest rates of domestic violence homicides (for all
genders) and is among the top ten for women killed by men.[3] "Some
of these women have suffered horrific abuse from boyfriends, fa-
thers and some their brothers and others their own mothers. And
know themselves to be survivors now, not victims. I am lucky to be
alive myself."[4]

It's not just Oklahoma. In 1999, the US Department of Justice
found that nearly half of all women in local jails and state prisons

had experienced abuse before their arrests. More recent studies indicate that the prevalence of abuse has not abated. A 2016 report by the Vera Institute of Justice found that, while approximately 33 percent of women in the United States have experienced violence at the hands of an intimate partner, that rate more than doubles to 77 percent among incarcerated women.[5] Eighty-six percent of incarcerated women experienced sexual violence (either at the hands of a partner or another person).

No one knows how many abuse survivors are imprisoned for defending themselves or for actions that they were coerced into by abusive partners. Similarly, no governmental agency tracks how many survivors are incarcerated for actions committed by their abusers.

Isolated studies provide snapshots. A 1977 study in Chicago's Cook County Jail found that 40 percent of women charged with murdering their partners reported that their partners had been abusive. Each woman had called police at least five times; many had already separated from that partner in an attempt to escape. Thirty years later, a study by the New York prison system found that, of women convicted of killing someone close to them, 67 percent had been abused by that person.[6] A 2011 report found that 93 percent of women convicted of killing an intimate partner had a history of domestic and/or sexual violence during their adult years.[7]

For years, the intersections between women's histories of violence and their imprisonment remained largely ignored in policy discussions about the criminal legal system.

These intersections began to draw national attention in 2012 when Marissa Alexander, a Black mother living in Jacksonville, Florida, was sentenced to twenty years after firing a warning shot to ward off her attacking husband. In 2010, Alexander, who had given birth to a premature baby girl nine days earlier, was at home when her husband, Rico Gray, attacked her. "He assaulted me, shoving, strangling and holding me against my will, preventing me from fleeing all while I begged for him to leave," Alexander recounted in an open letter.[8]

She fled to the garage but realized she had forgotten the keys to her truck. The garage door opener didn't work, forcing her to return inside. She did, grabbing her (legally registered) gun. She intended to either leave through another door or grab her phone to call for help. Gray charged at her; in response, Alexander fired a warning shot. Gray left and called the police, who arrested Alexander and charged her with aggravated assault with a deadly weapon.

Florida has a stand-your-ground law that permits a person to fight back against an aggressor if they believe they are in imminent danger. During a pretrial hearing, Alexander tried to argue self-defense under that law, but the judge ruled that Alexander could have left her own home. In a sixty-six-page deposition, Gray admitted to abusing not only Alexander but also the other four women with whom he had children. At trial, witnesses, including several family members, testified about the injuries that Gray had inflicted on her. Gray's sisters-in-law also testified that he had a reputation for violence in the community. Nonetheless, the judge instructed the jury that, when considering whether Alexander had acted in self-defense, she had to prove beyond a reasonable doubt that Gray was in the process of committing aggravated battery when she fired the gun.

The stories of abuse that Alexander endured did not seem to move the jury, who deliberated for twelve minutes before voting to convict her. In Florida, the prosecutor has the discretion to add a sentencing enhancement of ten or more years if a gun was used. (Florida's 10-20-Life law requires a minimum sentence of ten, twenty, or twenty-five years to life for certain felonies involving a firearm.) The prosecutor chose to exercise that discretion, and Alexander was sentenced to twenty years in prison. (Ironically, or perhaps tellingly, the same prosecutor, Angela Corey, would later fail to convict George Zimmerman for fatally shooting seventeen-year-old Trayvon Martin. Unlike Alexander, Zimmerman was allowed to argue, according to the stand-your-ground law, that he had killed the teenager in an act of self-defense. He was acquitted.)

Similar stories can be found in prisons across the country. The National Clearinghouse for the Defense of Battered Women, which provides support to abuse survivors who are going through criminal court proceedings as well as survivors who have been convicted and imprisoned, receives over a thousand letters each year from survivors in prison across the country. "Some letters start with 'I'm on my 35th year in prison,'" said founder and director Sue Osthoff.[9]

For many, their odyssey through the legal system—from the police precinct to the courtrooms and even to the prison—is riddled with dismissals of the violence they endured. In many cases, attempts to introduce histories of abuse, trauma, and violence as part of a legal defense are dismissed as the "abuse excuse."

That's what happened to Kelly Ann Savage, whose husband killed her three-year-old son, Justin, from a previous relationship. Savage had a plan to escape her abusive husband; she had bus tickets for herself and her children to leave their small town for her sister's home in Los Angeles. But fifteen hours before the bus was scheduled to leave, her husband fatally beat the toddler. Both parents were arrested and charged with first-degree murder.

In court, the prosecutor used her history of abuse to argue that Savage enjoyed being beaten, that she allowed her husband to beat Justin in order to please him, and that, because she had not fled, she was equally at fault for her son's death. Her attorney employed a psychologist as a defense witness, but the psychologist was not an expert in battered women's syndrome or domestic violence. Instead, she testified that Savage had post-traumatic stress disorder stemming from a history of childhood abuse and that people suffering from PTSD sometimes block out or fail to hear signs of danger.

Both parents were convicted of torture and first-degree murder and sentenced to life without the possibility of parole. In 1998, nearly three years after her son's death—years that she spent in jail—Savage entered California's prison system.[10] There, she began the path of healing, including becoming certified as a peer educator for domestic violence and sexual assault.

As she facilitated support groups for survivors, Savage found that approximately 70 percent of the women around her had also experienced abuse. She recalled one class of forty-nine women in which only four reported they had no abuse in their homes before the age of eighteen. Of those four, only one said that she had also never experienced abuse during her adult life.

Abuse also plays a significant role in twenty-nine states where a woman need not even have participated in a crime to be charged. In those states, she can be charged for *not* acting under "failure to protect" laws that allow prosecutors to charge mothers if an abusive partner or caregiver hurts their child. The penalty for failing to protect is equal to and sometimes even greater than the penalty for actually inflicting harm on the child.

That's what happened to Tondalo Hall, a young Black mother and domestic violence survivor in Oklahoma. In 2006, her boyfriend, Robert Braxton Jr., broke the ribs and femur of her three-month-old daughter. He pleaded guilty and was sentenced to ten years in prison; eight of those years were suspended. He spent only two years behind bars.[11]

Despite testifying against her boyfriend and presenting evidence of his past abuse, Hall was sentenced to two consecutive fifteen-year prison sentences.[12] In 2019, an outpouring of public outrage, support, and pressure resulted in the governor commuting, or shortening, her sentence, allowing her to be released early. By then, Hall had spent fifteen years behind bars.[13]

As awareness about domestic violence increases, the myth of the "abuse excuse" is slowly beginning to crumble. Advocates who work with incarcerated domestic violence survivors are using the growing awareness to push legislation to free them—and to keep others out of prison altogether.

In 2012, California passed two laws, popularly known as the Sin by Silence laws. The first allowed imprisoned abuse survivors to file a legal motion challenging their incarceration if their original trial lacked or had only limited expert testimony about abuse; the second required the parole board to seriously consider evidence of abuse instead of interpreting it as a person's failure to take responsibility for their actions.

In 2016, Illinois passed the Corrections-Mitigating Factor law directing judges to consider the role of abuse during sentencing procedures. Abuse survivors who had already been sentenced and imprisoned could petition for resentencing if evidence of abuse was not considered during their initial sentencing hearing. Three years later, in 2019, nineteen petitions had been filed in Cook County. Two of those petitions resulted in a reduced sentence. Another thirteen petitions were filed in counties outside of Chicago. But just because the law has been passed doesn't mean that prosecutors are on board: in at least twelve of these cases, prosecutors have filed motions to have these petitions dismissed.[14]

In May 2019, after a decade of organizing by formerly and currently incarcerated women, New York passed the Domestic Violence Survivors Justice Act. The act allows judges to depart from sentencing guidelines if abuse was directly related to the crime. In practice, that means that judges can issue sentences that are significantly shorter or divert a survivor from prison altogether.

For survivors who have already been sentenced and imprisoned, the act allows them to petition for resentencing if they can provide evidence that the abuse was a significant factor in their crime.[15] The act applies not only to survivors who harmed their abusers but also to those who were coerced into crimes by their partners. If the statistics from the 1999 Department of Justice report still hold true, the act could affect approximately 185 women and 175 men currently in New York State prisons and approximately 365 women and 115 men facing abuse-related criminal charges each year.[16]

In one of the first hearings after the law took effect, the judge decided against applying the law's sentencing provisions to twenty-six-year-old Taylor Partlow, whose manslaughter trial included five witness testimonies about the abuse she had suffered at the hands of her boyfriend. "The abuse, number one, was not substantial abuse and not a significant contributing factor to your behavior," he said at the sentencing hearing. "But I do agree there was domestic abuse."[17] Despite his declaration, the judge sentenced her to eight years in prison, the sentence suggested for manslaughter under the Domestic Violence Survivors Justice Act. Under the state's sentencing guidelines, the judge could have sentenced Partlow to twenty-five years in prison.

Advocates are also organizing to free incarcerated survivors in other ways. Organizers working around the intersections of prison and gender violence in various parts of the country have formed Survived and Punished, a coalition that both provides support for incarcerated survivors and raises public awareness about the issues.

In August 2017, Chicago organizers affiliated with Survived and Punished met with the assistant attorney under the newly elected prosecutor Kim Foxx, who campaigned as a progressive prosecutor and became the first Black female district attorney in Chicago. Organizers brought the cases of Naomi Freeman, Caress Shumaker, and Paris Knox, three Black domestic violence survivors who were facing criminal charges for the deaths of their abusive loved ones.

The Chicago organizers talked about the prosecution—and eventual freeing—of Marissa Alexander in Jacksonville, Florida, and noted that, like Alexander, the three Chicago women had also endured severe violence at the hands of their partners. Among the organizers were abuse survivors who had themselves been through the criminal legal system; they shared their stories of encountering violence first from their loved ones and then from the legal system. Their stories touched the attorney; within months, the prosecutor's office dropped the charges against Shumaker, reduced the first-degree charges against Freeman to involuntary manslaughter with a sentence of thirty months of probation and no prison time, and offered Knox, who had already served thirteen years of a forty-year prison sentence for first-degree murder, a plea deal for second-degree murder with time served. She was released on February 15, 2018.[18]

In New York, organizers have targeted Governor Andrew Cuomo, who, in 2015, announced that his office would review the sentences of people imprisoned throughout the state. Those who had shown remorse and rehabilitation would be granted clemency in the form of a commutation, or a shortening, of their prison sentence. The following year, he granted clemency to Valerie Seeley, an abuse survivor who had served sixteen years of a nineteen-to-life sentence for the death of her abusive boyfriend; his action allowed her to go home in 2017, two years before her earliest parole date. As of May 2020, she is one of only two abuse survivors to whom Cuomo has granted clemency.

In response, advocates have formed #FreeThemNY, a campaign to push the governor to grant clemency to domestic violence survivors incarcerated for defending themselves. They have visited and collected the stories of imprisoned abuse survivors, circulated petitions urging the governor to grant clemency, held rallies outside his office and his fundraising events, and raised visibility about how society's failure to stop domestic violence leads to incarceration. After the passage of the Domestic Violence Survivors Justice Act, advocates began working with incarcerated survivors to file petitions for resentencing hearings.

Despite these efforts, many survivors trapped in the nation's legal system are still confronted with the myth of the abuse excuse when they attempt to introduce their experiences of violence. This myth allows society to ignore not only the pervasive violence against women but also society's failures to address and build resources to eradicate domestic violence.

CHAPTER 13

Mass incarceration and immigrant detention are unrelated issues that can be addressed separately.

They call immigrant detention civil confinement, but prison is prison no matter what label you use, and prison breaks people's souls, hearts, and even minds.

—MALIK NDAULA, who had been imprisoned by ICE[1]

Conversations about mass incarceration typically disregard the tens of thousands of people in immigrant detention because detention is considered a civil, not criminal, form of custody. People are detained on civil violations, such as overstaying their work or travel visa. Though confinement is civil, conditions mimic those inside jails and prisons—people are locked inside, guarded by officers who have the power to further restrict their movements and to punish them for the slightest infraction, and told when to wake, eat, and move.

But that conversational omission has started to change in recent years, especially as detention numbers have soared in the wake of Trump's anti-immigration policies. Advocates and organizers, including those who have been detained themselves, have been raising awareness about the conditions in immigrant detention as well as the overlap between those who are impacted by the criminal legal system and those impacted by the immigration system.

As with jails and prisons, police are often the starting point for immigrant detention. In some states, police are allowed to demand a person's immigration papers. Immigrants who are jailed, no matter how minor the charge, are subject to Secure Communities, a partnership between local law enforcement and immigration officials. Under Secure Communities, local authorities run each person's fingerprints through federal immigration databases; immigration authorities can then place a hold on immigrants who might otherwise be released.

As of 2019, over fifty-one thousand immigrants are in detention on any given day. How did we get to this point?

Before 2002, immigration enforcement was controlled by the Immigration and Naturalization Service, an agency under the Department of Justice. In response to the attacks on the World Trade Center on September 11, 2001, Congress passed the 2002 Homeland Security Act, which created the US Immigration and Customs Enforcement (ICE). The agency became part of the newly created Department of Homeland Security and was granted a combination of civil and criminal authority to enforce federal laws governing border control, customs, trade, and immigration.

But even before 2002, Congress had passed laws mandating deportation for those who had been convicted of misdemeanors and felonies. In 1986, Congress passed the Immigration Reform and Control Act, which made noncitizens with criminal convictions subject to deportation. The act created two programs that allowed immigration officials to search jails and prisons for immigrants who could be deported. Those two programs would later be consolidated into the 2006 Criminal Alien Program.

In 1996, Congress expanded the list of deportable offenses and mandated detention with the Antiterrorism and Effective Death Penalty Act (AEDPA) and the Illegal Immigration Reform and Immigration Responsibility Act (IIRIRA).

AEDPA required the mandatory detention of noncitizens who had been convicted of a wide range of charges, including minor drug charges. It also expanded the category of aggravated felonies that subject immigrants to deportations. Aggravated felonies had previously only encompassed murder and felony trafficking in drugs or firearms. Under the expanded definition, aggravated felonies now refer to convictions that need not be serious, dangerous, or even felonies, but they still carry serious immigration consequences. Aggravated felonies now include over thirty types of offenses ranging from murder and assault to filing a false tax return and failing to appear in court.

IIRIRA further expanded the list of acts that mandated detention. Under these acts, judges could no longer consider a person's circumstances, including their family and community ties or the severity of their offense.

These acts drastically increased the number of immigrants in detention: in 1994, approximately 6,785 people were in detention on any given day. By 2001, that number had more than tripled to a daily average of 20,429. By 2008, that average had reached more than 31,000 people.[2]

The 1986 Immigration Reform and Control Act created two programs allowing immigration officials access to jails and prisons to search for immigrants who are deemed deportable. In 2006, ICE consolidated these two programs into the Criminal Alien Program (CAP), ICE's largest deportation program, which is responsible for between two-thirds and three-quarters of all deportations from within the US (or deportations that did not happen at the border). The intersections of criminalization and immigrant detention are sometimes referred to as "crimmigration."[3]

Like the term "aggravated felonies," the Criminal Alien Program is a misnomer. Approximately half a million people were deported under CAP between 2010 and 2013; over 27 percent had no criminal conviction. The second- and third-biggest categories were of people whose "most serious" criminal conviction involved a "traffic offense" (20 percent) and "dangerous drugs" (18 percent).[4] This means that an immigrant who pleaded guilty during the height of the drug war is now deportable. So is an immigrant who was jailed for nearly any reason, however minor.

At the same time, Congress changed unauthorized border crossing from a civil offense to one that was punishable with years of imprisonment followed by deportation. Prosecutions for unauthorized entry skyrocketed—from less than 4,000 in 1992 to 31,000 in 2004. That number nearly tripled to 91,000 prosecutions in 2013 alone.[5]

In 2009, Congress passed a mandate that, at any given time, ICE "maintain a level of not less than 33,400 detention beds" as part of its appropriations act. That level was increased to 34,000 in 2015. Meanwhile, under the slogan of "families, not felons," the Obama administration justified its continued criminalization, detention, and deportation of nearly three million immigrants during his tenure, earning him the moniker "deporter-in-chief."

That's the backstory of the groundwork for today's unprecedented number of people in immigrant detention. Today the thousands of people who are caught crossing the US-Mexico border without authorization are charged with a misdemeanor or felony. They're sent to government-run facilities known as *hieleros*, or ice boxes (to denote both the cold temperatures inside and the ICE agency), before being sent to a detention center or jail. There is no mandate that people be confined close to their family and community—they can be shipped to any of the nearly two hundred detention centers or jails run by or contracted by ICE across the country.

Under Trump's presidency, the number of people in ICE detention has skyrocketed from approximately thirty-four thousand in 2016, the last year of Obama's presidency, to over fifty-one thousand in 2019.[6]

The rate of women's detention has increased over the past three years as well. In April 2016, 14.6 percent of all people detained by ICE, or 4,829, were women. During the first four months of 2017, the number of immigration arrests of women rose by 35 percent. As of late 2018, 21 percent of people in ICE detention were women.

It's unclear whether this figure includes trans women.[7] ICE has a trans-specific housing unit in New Mexico's Cibola County, though it has also detained trans women in men's detention facilities.

During the first four months of 2017, ICE detained 292 pregnant women, reversing the Obama-era policy to release immigrants who were pregnant.[8] Under Trump, ICE has also continued the Obama-era policy of detaining children with their parents at family detention centers, whereas unaccompanied children are detained in shelters run by nonprofit organizations.

Approximately 73 percent of people (26,249 individuals) in immigrant detention are confined in facilities owned and operated by private prison corporations.[9] (In contrast, as discussed in chapter 4, private prison corporations hold only 8.5 percent of the US prison population.)[10] Many ICE contracts with private corporations use either a fixed rate or a daily rate per person detained. These per diems range from $60 to $120.[11]

Some immigrants are even detained in former jails and prisons. In 2019, private prison corporation GEO Group, for instance, bought and repurposed a 1990s women's prison in Basile, Louisiana.[12] Now that same prison holds approximately one thousand immigrants awaiting deportation hearings.

ICE also detains approximately twenty-two thousand people in county jails.[13] As more states implement reforms to the criminal bail system, in which people are no longer required to pay exorbitant bail amounts to ensure their pretrial freedom, county jails have been turning to ICE to fill their empty jail beds with detained immigrants.[14] Many jails place detained immigrants in solitary confinement, ostensibly for their own protection rather than because they pose a threat to anyone's safety.

Furthermore, many of these jails are located in counties where only a sliver of the population, if any, speak the language of those detained. In Baldwin County, Alabama, for instance, only 2.5 percent of the town's 9,300 residents are Latinx, while more than 90 percent of people detained in the jail are from Mexico or Latin

America.[15] In some facilities, whether county jails or larger detention centers located in predominantly white rural areas, staff members chastise immigrants for not speaking English, call them racist and derogatory names, and abuse them physically or sexually.

Adults in ICE detention face similar conditions and abuses as those in nonimmigrant jails and prisons. They are not allowed freedom of movement. Instead, as in jails and prisons, they are confined in dorms or cells with all movements strictly controlled. Phone calls are not free; in fact, they're often exorbitantly expensive. Family and community members cannot freely visit; instead, they must adhere to visiting hours set by the institution. Food is often inadequate. Many have reported waiting up to seven hours between meals and being served food that is sometimes spoiled or contains hair, plastic, bugs, rocks, or mice.[16] As in jails and prisons, detained immigrants must often supplement their meager fare with the (often unhealthy and overpriced) snacks for sale at the commissary, or prison store.

As with jails and prisons, medical care in immigrant detention is frequently inadequate. Many immigrants have reported waiting several weeks before they are able to see a medical provider, and many reported not receiving needed medications, including HIV medications.[17] This neglect has led to deaths that could have been prevented. The 1,500-bed Stewart Detention Center in rural Georgia, for instance, has had four deaths in custody between 2017 and 2019.[18]

In over twenty-five facilities, immigrants are paid one dollar a day to scrub toilets, mop floors, do laundry, or prepare meals as part of ICE's Voluntary Work Program.[19] Under the program, ICE reimburses immigrant detention centers exactly one dollar a day for each person who worked eight or more hours. It's a rate set by Congress in 1950, codified in the 1978 Appropriations Act and not raised since then. These paltry wages allow detained people to purchase phone cards to call their families or their attorneys or to buy food at the commissary.

Like other aspects of immigrant detention, the title of the Voluntary Work Program is misleading. Nearly half a dozen lawsuits have been filed by people detained in facilities around the country; these suits accuse staff of punishing detained workers who attempt to take a day off, complain about not being paid more (or not being paid at all), or balk at working additional hours by locking them in their cells all day, threatening to move them to more dangerous housing units, and/or withholding soap, shampoo, and feminine hygiene supplies. By coercing detained people to work under such threats, the suits argue, these facilities are violating federal statutes against human trafficking (which is defined by involuntary labor obtained through "force, fraud or coercion").[20]

Not every detention center participates in the Voluntary Work Program. In fact, many do not, but that doesn't mean these facilities don't rely on detained immigrants to perform these same tasks. Instead of being paid, they are allowed more time out of their cells, greater access to the law library and recreation yards, and larger portions of food.

In past years, discussions about mass incarceration have remained separate from those about immigration detention and deportation. That's beginning to change—and organizers working on both issues have sometimes joined forces to fight against crimmigration policies. In New York City, for instance, ICE had an office at Rikers Island where immigration officials would meet with and interview immigrants who had been arrested and jailed pending trial to see if they might be eligible for deportation. Organizers working on immigrant rights and criminal justice reform formed the ICE Out of Rikers Coalition. In 2011, the group succeeded in passing the first city law that limited the jail system's cooperation with ICE. In 2014, in response to sustained organizing and lobbying by ICE Out of Rikers, the city council passed legislation that drastically limited the circumstances under which police and the jail system are allowed to honor immigration detainers. The following year, in 2015, the ICE office at Rikers Island was closed.

It's important to recognize the similarities between the criminal legal and the immigrant detention systems—both seek to surveil, control, and confine people who are considered undesirable or "disposable" to US society. Both are systems that degrade, dehumanize, and torture people with their conditions of confinement. Both rip apart families and sow terror in individuals and communities. Both operate with a lack of transparency and accountability. At the same time, as explored in chapter 15, people confined in both systems organize and resist these conditions in various ways, from filing lawsuits to hunger and work strikes. Conversations about mass incarceration need to acknowledge and include immigrant detention.

PART 4

How Do We End Mass Incarceration?

CHAPTER 14

Most people are in prison for nonviolent drug offenses. Let them out and we'll end mass incarceration.

To truly tackle mass incarceration, we need to move beyond talking only about nonviolent drug offenses and challenge lawmakers—and ourselves—to include the more complicated and nuanced scenarios involving violence.

If every person incarcerated for drug offenses were released tomorrow, that still leaves over 1.2 million people in prison.

Mary Fish has been in and out of prison for nearly forty years. Her legal troubles began in 1979 when the twenty-seven-year-old Oklahoma mother drove her brother, recently released from prison, to a local bar to cash a check. There, she was groped by another patron and kicked out by the bartender so she drove away without her brother. When she returned for her brother, she saw police surrounding him. Her brother waved at her to keep driving; Fish made a U-turn, an act that caused one of the officers to assume she was going to hit him, though she did not. After a car chase through town, Fish was nonetheless arrested and charged with assault and battery with an automobile.[1]

She was sentenced to one year in prison and released after serving seven months. It was her first time in prison, but it would not be her last. In 1981, Fish was living in a trailer, growing marijuana, and drowning her grief about her mother's death in a bottle. Three men visited her to buy marijuana; two left after the sale, but one stayed behind and drank with Fish until she passed out. She woke to find the man on top of her. She tried to flee, but he caught up to her; she then stabbed him with a paring knife. He died and she was sentenced to ten years in prison for first-degree manslaughter. In prison, a cellmate introduced her to Dilaudid, a pain reliever. "I thought if I could just stop drinking, I could lick this curse that would not leave me," Fish recalled. But instead, she recounted, "I turned from an alcoholic to a Dilaudid-injecting addict." Upon release, her new addiction led to more drug use and more arrests, mostly for minor offenses like shoplifting.

In 2002, her drug use led her to brutally beat a man after he verbally threatened her ten-year-old son. She was convicted of assault and battery with intent to kill and, because she had taken his wallet, robbery. She was sentenced to forty years in prison.[2]

Except for the first, all of Fish's arrests and incarcerations stem from alcohol or substance use. All are also violent offenses. Yet Fish, and so many others with similar stories, are excluded from the narrative that mass incarceration is driven by nonviolent drug offenses.

When talking about ways to decrease the number of people behind bars, advocates and politicians often focus on people imprisoned for nonviolent drug convictions. Let them out, goes the popular wisdom, and we'll have ended mass incarceration. It's an easier sell to a public still worried about crime and violence, but the numbers don't add up.

The reality is that, while draconian drug laws have played a role in the skyrocketing number of prisoners, focusing solely on nonviolent drug offenses won't substantially decrease our nation's prison population or end mass incarceration.

In 2017, more than half of the people in state prisons (709,700 individuals) were serving time for violent offenses. Murder accounted for 14.3 percent (182,200 individuals) of convictions.[3] People with drug convictions accounted for only a slightly higher percentage (14.4 percent, or 183,900 people) in state prisons.[4]

The myth that mass incarceration is caused by nonviolent drug offenses is rooted in some of the laws that helped fuel the prison explosion. But nonviolent drug offenses have never been the sole cause.

Between 1990 and 2000, the number of people sent to prison nearly doubled, from 771,423 to 1,381,892.[5] Much of this growth has been attributed to draconian drug laws and mandatory sentencing laws, the latter requiring that the judge sentence a convicted person to a fixed term in prison. Judges are not allowed to make exceptions, to consider mitigating circumstances, or to impose less severe penalties, including shorter prison sentences or nonprison sentences, such as probation or drug treatment.

In 1973, New York passed the Rockefeller Drug Laws. Named after then governor Nelson Rockefeller, these laws required judges to issue a prison sentence of fifteen years to life for anyone convicted of selling two ounces or possessing four ounces of narcotics. During sentencing, they were not allowed the discretion to consider whether this was a person's first offense or to consider the circumstances of their arrest. That year, New York held 13,437 people in its prisons; twenty years later, that number had more than quadrupled to 64,569.

Other states followed suit. While many of the mandatory sentencing laws revolved around drug offenses, some also tied the hands of judges in non-drug cases. In 1993, Washington State passed the nation's first three-strikes law, in which any person convicted of a third felony was automatically sentenced to life in prison.

The following year, fueled by the kidnapping and murder of twelve-year-old Polly Klaas by a man who had been paroled months earlier, California passed its own three-strikes law. California's law mandated that a person convicted of a second felony be sentenced to twice the amount of prison time than if it had been their first felony. If convicted of a third felony, twenty-five years to life was the automatic sentence.

Within a decade, California courts sentenced over 80,000 people convicted of a second felony and 7,500 convicted of a third felony to these mandatory prison terms. By December 2004, nearly 43,000 people (26 percent of the state's prison population) were imprisoned under the three-strikes law.[6] Over one-third (37 percent) were convicted of a crime against a person (robbery, assault with a deadly weapon, or assault and battery) while less than one-quarter (23 percent) were convicted of drug offenses (possessing or selling drugs).

In 1999, Florida passed and enacted its 10-20-Life law, which allowed prosecutors to add a sentencing enhancement to any conviction that involved firearms. This meant a mandatory ten-year sentence if a person displayed a gun, a mandatory twenty years if a gun was fired (even if it was fired as a warning shot and not at an individual), and twenty-five years if someone was wounded. The law did not allow the judge to consider mitigating circumstances or exceptions. The law was repealed in 2016, but during its seventeen years in effect, more than fifteen thousand people had been sentenced under the enhancement.[7] (The repeal is not retroactive, meaning that those who had previously been sentenced and were still imprisoned had to serve the entirety of their sentence.)

It's not just mandatory sentences that have caused prison populations to skyrocket. For decades, even in cases where mandatory sentences do not apply, prosecutors and judges are often reluctant to appear soft on crime by considering mitigating circumstances or seeking non-prison sanctions. Prosecutors have the discretion of whether to bring criminal charges against a person and what those charges might be. In 1980, for instance, when Richard Sinnott, then an investigator for the Suffolk County District Attorney's office, was arrested for shooting a US Coast Guardsman on the street; the district attorney chose not to bring charges against him. But as a judge, Sinnott was unwilling to extend the same leniency to those who appeared in his court. Nearly forty years later, when the current district attorney attempted to exercise her prosecutorial discretion and drop misdemeanor charges against a group of people arrested while protesting a 2019 Straight Pride march, Sinnott refused the DA's request. He ordered one person held on $750 bail and one of the defense attorneys jailed for contempt of court when she objected.[8]

Both district attorneys and judges are elected officials and often want to avoid being seen as soft on crime. They're not the only politicians who view leniency as a potential death knell to their political aspirations. Throughout the 1980s and 1990s, lawmakers seemed to be running a race to see who could be toughest on crime. Desperate to avoid accusations of being too lenient, legislators pushed for increasingly harsher punishments, leading to a skyrocketing of the nation's prison population.

Now, faced with overcrowded prisons, their exorbitant price tags, and growing opposition to "lock-em-up" policies, politicians are beginning to replace tough-on-crime stances with (limited) criminal justice reform measures. But these reforms largely focus on people convicted of nonviolent offenses and, even if all are enacted, won't end mass incarceration.

Voters, too, have shown their fatigue with the lock-em-up policies of previous years. In 2012, California voters passed Proposition 36, which allowed resentencing people whose third strike was not considered violent or serious. The proposition didn't open the floodgates of the state's prisons: only one-third of the nine thousand people sentenced to a third strike qualified for a rehearing. The other six thousand, who had violent convictions, did not.[9]

In 2018, Congress passed the First Step Act, a federal bill that was widely hailed as bipartisan criminal justice reform. The act included changes to sentencing laws to allow judges more flexibility in passing sentences below mandatory minimums for nonviolent drug offenders and in reducing mandatory minimums associated with the three-strikes law. But the act only applies to people in federal prisons—180,000 of the 2.1 million behind bars (13 percent of the country's prison population)—and then only a fraction of them. Aside from those who already qualify under the 2010 Fair Sentencing Act, the First Step Act does not extend sentencing reductions retroactively; those sentenced before 2018 remain stuck serving draconian amounts of time. Furthermore, undocumented immigrants are not given access to expanded rehabilitative programs and services like halfway houses. Instead, they are fed into immigrant detention and deportation.

These bipartisan reforms and sentencing changes that are focused on nonviolent drug charges won't change the predicament for many behind bars. These drug policy changes will help some but will still fail tens of thousands of others currently locked away; they also do not stop thousands more from being locked up in the future.

As of 2018, less than 22 percent of the 1.5 million people incarcerated in state and federal prisons have been convicted of drug offenses.[10] If every person incarcerated for drug offenses were released tomorrow, that still leaves over 1.2 million people in prison.

In contrast, nearly half (731,000) of these 1.5 million incarcerated people have been convicted of violent acts. These people are often ignored during public conversations about reducing prison populations. That's because their stories are frequently messy, complicated, and include victims who have been harmed or killed.

Take Betsy Ramos, for instance. Drug policy is one of the causes of her decades-long incarceration, but that's not why she's currently in prison. Ramos had three previous drug convictions, including a federal conviction and a three-year prison sentence for bringing heroin into the United States from Colombia. While in prison, she learned that she had HIV, a diagnosis that stunned and devastated her. Upon release, she was sent to a halfway house where she met Joseph Serrano, who had recently been released from state prison. Serrano, who had his own history of drug-related arrests, told her he would love and accept her even with her HIV diagnosis. But he soon used the diagnosis as a means of control, repeatedly telling her that no one else would love her. He controlled what she wore and isolated her from the outside world. He also beat and sexually assaulted her.[11]

Drug use is common among women who have experienced violence and trauma.[12] It was the coping mechanism that Ramos turned to. Her boyfriend, Serrano, used drugs, too, and, at one point, was arrested for drug possession. He failed to show up for court and a judge issued a warrant for his arrest. In May 1998, when two police officers arrived at her door, Ramos was too afraid not to obey Serrano's demand to hide him. She did hide him, but the officers still found the man. Serrano grabbed one officer's gun and shot the other before being fatally shot. Ramos was arrested for the officer's murder. The media highlighted her past drug convictions, labeling her an "ex-con" and a "convicted drug dealer and smuggler."[13] The jury acquitted her of the murder and gun charges but convicted her of second-degree manslaughter. The judge sentenced her to fifteen years to life, which meant that, after serving fifteen years in prison, she was able to appear before the parole board. She did so four times. Each time, she was denied parole. On her fifth hearing, after twenty-one years behind bars, she was granted parole. But, because she had been on federal probation when she was arrested that fatal May morning, she was immediately transferred to a federal prison to serve a two-year sentence for violating her probation.

Violence and drugs are often a pathway to prison for women. Their rap sheet may list charges that provoke fear—murder, manslaughter, attempted murder, assault. But, as Ramos's story illustrates, their experiences are frequently more nuanced and complicated than a three-minute evening news clip or a click-bait headline.

Ramos was one of 34,000 people in women's state prisons convicted of violent crimes. Murder makes up nearly one-third of those convictions. In contrast, women with drug convictions account for 24 percent (or 22,000 women) in state prisons and 7,400 in the federal system. That's a total of 29,400 women sentenced to prison for drug crimes. Focusing solely on them excludes nearly two-thirds of the women's prison population.

Focusing solely on drug policy reform is not enough. To truly tackle mass incarceration, we need to move beyond talking only about nonviolent drug offenses and challenge lawmakers—and ourselves—to include the more complicated and nuanced scenarios involving violence.

CHAPTER 15

People in prison don't resist or organize against abusive conditions.

We felt it was time to speak up, make a
stand, and be heard.

—SISSY, incarcerated in Alabama

The media and historians continue to neglect the topic of resistance and organizing behind bars. That's in large part because prison walls are designed to keep people—and information—from getting out.

The most famous prison rebellion occurred in 1971. On September 9, fed up with the brutal conditions at New York's maximum-security prison in Attica, incarcerated men seized control of the prison, taking forty-three staff members hostage. They issued twenty-seven demands, including educational programs, fair parole processes, and an end to racism and violence by the majority white staff.[1] The uprising garnered the attention and support of outside activists and organizers, who acted as intermediaries between the incarcerated men and state officials. Four days later, on September 13, then governor Nelson Rockefeller ordered state troopers to quell the uprising. The troopers fired tear gas and then bullets into the yard where many incarcerated people and their hostages were gathered. Thirty-nine people—including ten hostages—died; numerous others were injured, both during the retaking and the subsequent brutal beating of those who had rebelled.

Forty years later, in July 2011, hundreds of men imprisoned in California's Pelican Bay State Prison launched a mass hunger strike. Many had spent years—and some had spent decades—locked into windowless eleven-by-seven-foot cells for twenty-two to twenty-four hours each day. The hunger strikers issued five demands, including an end to long-term solitary confinement, changes to the criteria for placement in Pelican Bay, and adequate and nutritious food. Over a thousand imprisoned at Pelican Bay and another six thousand across the state refused to eat for three weeks. They struck again for three weeks in September 2011, and in 2012 they filed a lawsuit challenging the state's solitary confinement policies.

In 2013, dissatisfied with the lack of promised changes, they launched another hunger strike. On the first day, nearly thirty thousand people imprisoned across the state refused food.[2] The strike lasted for sixty days, though the number of participants dwindled over time. In 2015, prison officials agreed to a settlement limiting placement in Pelican Bay's isolation units to five years; the hundreds who had been held in isolation for ten or more years would be transferred to less restrictive units.[3]

What both the Attica rebellion and the Pelican Bay hunger strikes have in common—besides the fierce determination of those imprisoned to change conditions—is the amount of outside support and attention their actions garnered. The majority of actions by people in the nation's jails, prisons, and immigrant detention centers generally remain unnoticed by the larger public.

The advent of cell phones has allowed incarcerated people to circumvent the tight restrictions and monitoring of prison phones and correspondence to get word to the outside world. Cell phones are technically contraband, or prohibited, within jails and prisons, but they are smuggled in and used for a variety of purposes.

One of those purposes has been to let the larger public know about the conditions inside jails and prisons—and what people inside are doing to resist and organize. In 2016, for example, incarcerated organizer Kinetic Justice used a contraband cell phone to call national news show *Democracy Now!* from his solitary confinement cell at Alabama's Holman Correctional Facility. Justice told viewers about the upcoming ten-day work strike in the state's male prisons. The strikes were protesting the prisons' severe overcrowding, poor living conditions, and the Thirteenth Amendment of the Constitution, which allows unpaid labor as "punishment for a crime."[4] Other prison organizers have also used contraband cell phones to communicate with outside advocates and media, but because possessing a cell phone is against prison rules and can lead to solitary confinement, many are reluctant to publicly state this. Nevertheless, advocates and journalists have acknowledged that these calls allow them to learn about prison conditions and incarcerated people's actions, both of which might otherwise never be brought to their attention.

In 2020, as COVID-19 spread across jails, prisons, and detention centers nationwide, people inside resisted and rebelled to change the conditions that made them more vulnerable to contracting the virus. In dozens of jails, prisons, and detention centers across the country, people engaged in work strikes, hunger strikes, and even riots in attempts to get protective gear and cleaning supplies.[5]

As with many other aspects of mass incarceration, when prison organizing is recognized, the focus rests largely on the actions of incarcerated men. This is not because women behind bars don't organize. Instead, there are several reasons why women's actions are overlooked or not classified as resistance or organizing.

For one, when incarceration is viewed as an issue primarily affecting men, female-specific issues, such as parenting and child custody, sexual abuse by staff members, and reproductive healthcare, are often overlooked or ignored. Thus, the actions that women take to challenge and change these injustices are overlooked and ignored.

Second, women are often not part of the same outside networks and coalitions that support incarcerated men's organizing, leaving them excluded from calls for mass actions. For instance, women incarcerated at Alabama's Birmingham Work Release Center, where women are both imprisoned and allowed outside on work release, were unaware of the 2016 call for a statewide prison work strike—and unaware that any organizing had been taking place. "[I] never heard about a work strike and ask[ed] around. No one knew. Did it happen, do you know?" asked Sissy, who remains incarcerated there.[6]

If women do know and choose to participate in organized mass resistance—such as work or hunger strikes—they often lack the same networks of outside support to help them get the word out and prevent retaliation. For instance, in a Washington State women's prison, two women learned about a nationwide prison strike taking place on September 9, 2016. That day, they told their supervisor they were part of the work strike. Prison officials transferred them to the women's jail over two hundred miles across the state.

These obstacles haven't stopped women behind bars from engaging in hunger or work strikes. When the Trump administration dramatically increased the numbers of immigrants confined in detention centers, dozens embarked upon hunger strikes to demand better conditions inside and the opportunity to await (and fight) their deportation hearings from outside of detention. Among those dozens were women, many of them mothers separated from their children.

In 2017, more than thirty immigrant women detained at the Tacoma Northwest Detention Center outside Seattle embarked on a hunger strike that sparked a solidarity strike and encampment outside the detention center. They demanded an affordable bond (the equivalent of the criminal legal system's bail in which money is paid for temporary freedom pending court proceedings), political asylum, and improved conditions, including new underwear, improved medical care, and an end to staff throwing away their belongings.[7]

In June 2018, mothers detained at ICE's Port Isabel Service Processing Center in South Texas engaged in a rolling hunger strike, meaning that, for two weeks, fifteen mothers at a time embarked on a two- or three-day hunger strike. Another group began hunger striking when the first resumed eating. Though conditions in the detention center were atrocious—including poor food and lack of news from the outside world—these mothers were demanding the ability to call their children, from whom they had been separated under the Trump administration's zero tolerance policies.[8] Parenting is often not considered a prison issue—and thus not examined as a catalyst for prison organizing. In 2020, when a woman in a privately run ICE detention center in Basile, Louisiana, became ill, other detained women used the center's video-calling technology to stage a protest in which they described the conditions to the media, demanded protective gear, and held up handwritten signs stating "A woman here with us is very sick. She may have COVID-19." The women continued talking to the media until an officer noticed their actions, seized their posters, and ended the call.[9]

Finally, organizing in women's prisons, jails, and immigrant detention centers often looks different than what's typically thought of as in-prison organizing. In prisons, resistance can take the form of helping mothers navigate paperwork full of legal jargon to maintain custody of their children or organizing support groups addressing shared experiences of domestic, sexual, or familial violence, types of violence that are shared by up to 90 percent in any given women's prison. In some cases, these support groups have led to campaigns for mass clemencies. That's what happened in Ohio in the early 1990s after a support group for women serving lengthy prison sentences realized that many had been sentenced to life in prison for killing their abusive boyfriends or husbands. The group wrote a letter to the state governor asking him to consider commuting their sentences and inviting him to attend one of their weekly meetings so he could understand their circumstances. Then governor Richard Celeste sent one of his aides and his wife,

Dagmar, to the prison; after hearing their stories, both encouraged the women to apply for commutations. The women did, but they also decided not to limit their efforts to their support group. Instead, they reached out to other women in the prison, and if they, too, were incarcerated for killing their batterer, they helped them apply for commutation.

Talking to other women is not easy within prisons where movement is strictly limited. Want to go from the housing unit to the library? You need a pass for that. Want to go to the yard? You have to wait until your approved movement time—and that could be canceled at any time. Want to go to another housing unit to talk to the women there? That probably won't be permitted. But even with these restrictions, the women held in the Ohio prison found ways to reach out, and their efforts resulted in eighteen additional women applying for clemency. In the end, Celeste granted clemency to twenty-five women, shortening their sentences and allowing them to be released from prison. It was the first mass commutation of domestic violence survivors who had been incarcerated for killing their abusive partners.[10]

Organizing might also look like what Sissy and other women did to force authorities to address the rampant staff sexual abuse at Alabama's overcrowded, dilapidated Julia Tutwiler Prison for Women. Throughout the 1990s and early 2000s, women incarcerated there wrote letters to the US Department of Justice detailing the sexual abuse they either witnessed or personally experienced— and the repercussions if they attempted to report it. When the Justice Department launched a federal investigation, the women sent 233 more letters to federal officials to ensure these issues would be investigated.

The women also filed a lawsuit against both the State of Alabama and its Department of Corrections about the prison's overcrowding, extreme temperatures, and poor medical care. In response, a federal judge declared the prison unsafe and gave state officials thirty days to develop a plan to remedy conditions. The state's response was to contract with a private prison corporation to send 140 women to Basile, a small town in southwestern Louisiana more than seven hours away.[11]

The transfer led to even more organizing. After arriving in Basile, the women formed the Longtermers/Insiders group. "The group wanted to have a voice in the decision making," wrote Sissy. "We feared that once in Louisiana, we would be 'out of sight, out of mind.' . . . We felt it was time to speak up, make a stand, and be heard."[12]

The women worked together, helping each other develop the skills to produce a political platform about the overuse of women's incarceration, write articles for the local newspapers, write letters to legislative representatives, discuss legislation, and talk with people outside prison about advocating for them. "We . . . are continually striving to give input to a system that has not allowed us to be heard," Sissy wrote.[13]

Those efforts led Alabama lawmakers to establish the Commission on Girls and Women in the Criminal Justice System in 2006. The commission did a two-year study before issuing a series of recommendations, which included expanding the use of community-based alternatives to incarceration and closing and tearing down Tutwiler.[14] The following year, in 2007, the 140 women who had been moved to Basile, Louisiana, were transferred back to Tutwiler, which remains open (and overcrowded).

"If I could go back in time, would I do it again? Yes!" Sissy reflected. "I was part of something for a little while that had a voice even though it didn't last. It was there. And it paved the way for gender specific [issues] to be looked at in Alabama."[15]

Prison resistance and organizing can take many forms. Some, like riots, hunger strikes, and work strikes, are more likely to capture media and public attention; others, such as helping others with their legal work, organizing mass clemency campaigns, and repeatedly contacting outside agencies to draw attention to unjust or abusive conditions, often go unnoticed by the larger public.

CHAPTER 16

Prisons keep us safe from murderers and rapists.

Arrest and incarceration occur only after harm or violence has occurred; incarceration does not prevent these acts from happening.

❝W❞hat about the rapists? What about the murderers?"
Rape and murder are commonly invoked to justify the need for prisons. But in reality, arrest and incarceration occur only *after* harm or violence has occurred; incarceration does not prevent these acts from happening. It also doesn't guarantee justice or accountability for the survivor (or the survivor's loved ones).

Relying on prisons to prevent or address rape and violence ignores the reality that many acts of violence, particularly sexual violence, remain unreported. According to the Department of Justice, only 230 of every 1,000 sexual assaults are ever reported to the police.[1] In other words, three of four sexual assaults go unreported.[2]

From there, the numbers shrink even more drastically. Of those 230 sexual assaults that are reported to the police, only forty-six (or 20 percent) lead to arrest.[3] Of those forty-six arrests, only nine are referred to prosecutors and five ultimately result in a felony conviction.[4] Less than five of those convictions results in prison time.[5]

It's not necessarily the seriousness of the assault that is the deciding factor. As with all other aspects of the criminal legal system, men of color, particularly Black and Latinx men accused of raping white women, are treated more harshly than their white counterparts. Prosecutors are more likely to charge and juries more likely to convict men of color, particularly African American men (and boys). Just look at the Central Park Five, five Black and Latino teenagers between the ages of fourteen and sixteen who, in 1989, were accused of raping a white woman jogger. Police interrogated them, illegally, for hours. They coerced false confessions from four of the five teenagers who said they had been in the park during the assault. In court, the prosecutor seized on the coerced confessions to convince the jury to convict. But in 2002, the person who actually committed the rape confessed that he alone had committed the brutal sexual assault and beating. Though their convictions were vacated, all five men had already lost years of their lives behind bars.

At the same time, white men, particularly white men who sexually assault women of color, are more likely to be treated more leniently by the legal system. Just look at Brock Turner, the nineteen-year-old Stanford University swimmer who received a six-month jail sentence (and registration on the sex offender registry) after raping twenty-two-year-old Chanel Miller while she was unconscious. He served three months in county jail before being released to his parents' suburban home. (This is not to discount how life-long registration on the sex offender registry will forever affect his life. As will be discussed more in the following chapter, the hammer of the sex offender registry falls hardest on people of color: African Americans are disproportionately represented on the registry. They comprise 22 percent of those convicted of sex offenses but only 13 percent of the total US population.)[6]

Then there are those whose fame, fortune, and connections shield them from the full brunt of the criminal legal system. For decades, movie executive Harvey Weinstein sexually assaulted and coerced numerous actresses into sex. In 2015, after one actress complained that Weinstein had groped her, New York police set up a sting in which she recorded Weinstein making incriminating comments, including admitting to touching her breast without her consent. But the Manhattan district attorney declined to pursue charges, leaving Weinstein free to continue sexually abusing and exploiting Hollywood hopefuls. It was not until dozens of women came forward publicly accusing him of sexual harassment and assault that he was arrested on multiple sexual assault charges in May 2018; his nearly month-long trial ended with a conviction and a twenty-three-year sentence for criminal sexual acts and rape.[7]

Similarly, R&B singer R. Kelly sexually abused Black teenage girls for decades.[8] His predatory practices were known, but his fame and fortune shielded him for years. In 2002, Kelly was indicted on twenty-one counts of child pornography after police found videos of him engaging in sex with underage Black girls. He posted bail, went on with his life and continued to record music for the next six years before being acquitted at trial. In the ensuing years, other women came forward about the sexual abuse they suffered at his hands, leading to the documentary *Surviving R. Kelly*. In 2019, Kelly was arrested on several dozen counts of state and federal sexual misconduct charges in Illinois, Minnesota, and New York; as of May 2020, he was in a federal jail in Chicago awaiting these trials.[9]

The threat of imprisonment did not prevent either the movie mogul or the singer from abusing their celebrity to prey on women and girls; nor did it provide any sort of justice for the victims when they did turn to the court system.

Let's not forget, too, that violence, including sexual violence, can and does occur at the hands of law enforcement. When the assailant wears a badge, survivors are even more reluctant to come forward and report, a reluctance that allows police and other law enforcement to rape with impunity.

That was a fear that Oklahoma City police officer Daniel Holtzclaw wielded against at least thirteen Black women. Holtzclaw, who is white and Asian, specifically targeted Black women in low-income neighborhoods because he knew they would be too afraid to file a complaint. Many of the women had struggled with addiction, engaged in sex work, and/or had been arrested before, all issues they knew would make them less believable in the eyes of Holtzclaw's fellow law enforcement agents and investigators. Holtzclaw might have continued for years had he not sexually assaulted Jannie Liggons, a Black day care worker in her fifties. She reported the assault, prompting investigators to more closely examine another report, filed five weeks earlier, in which another Black woman said that a police officer had coerced her into oral sex. Police investigated further and found thirteen women who reported being raped by him.[10] He was convicted of raping eight women and sentenced to 263 years in prison.

Holtzclaw is an outlier only in that he was convicted and sentenced to over two centuries in prison. Sexual violence by law enforcement, however, is not rare. A 2015 investigation found that, over the course of six years, one thousand police officers throughout the country lost their badges because of sexual misconduct, including assault, rape, propositioning people for sex while on duty, or possessing child pornography.[11] We know about these officers because someone had the courage to report them, someone in a position of authority took the report seriously enough to investigate, *and* the officer lost their badge. But, just as sexual assault is underreported, sexual assault or abuse at the hands of police is also underreported, particularly because victims know that the word of an officer carries much more credibility among their peers, who are charged with investigating and prosecuting. Those one thousand officers who lost their badges are just a fraction of a number we may never know. What we do know is that even though they have sworn to uphold the law and put lawbreakers in prison, the threat of prison did not deter them.

There's also the fact that rape and sexual violence is more likely to happen at the hands of a known person. The Department of Justice found that stranger rape happens less than 20 percent of the time; the majority of rapes are committed by either an acquaintance (39 percent) or a current or former intimate partner (33 percent).[12] For children or teenagers, the number is even higher. Ninety-three percent knew the person who assaulted them—34 percent were family members, 59 percent were acquaintances, and only 7 percent were strangers.[13] In instances in which sexual violence is at the hands of a family member or other loved one, the threat of incarceration may actually deter the survivor from speaking out and having that person sent to prison.

Even if prisons don't prevent rapes from occurring, don't they deter murder?

Murder is a term that induces fear and panic, propping up the argument that prisons are necessary for safety. Again, it's important to remember that arrest, prosecution, and incarceration happen only *after* harm or violence has occurred. It does not prevent people from causing harm. Furthermore, not every murder results in an arrest, conviction, or incarceration. One-third of all homicides in the US remain unsolved.[14] For marginalized communities, the clearance rate is even higher: when it comes to the murders of Black men, nearly 35 percent remain unsolved (compared to 28 percent for murders of white men).[15] Clearance does not mean conviction; clearance simply means the police have identified the suspected killer. Clearance may result in an arrest or, if the person has died, simply a hypothesis.

The word "murder" conjures up images of violent monsters, leaving little room for nuance. But very few of the people currently incarcerated for murder or other acts of violence are one-dimensional sociopaths.

For instance, approximately 197,000 people (or 15 percent) in the nation's prisons have been convicted of murder or manslaughter.[16] Women make up nearly ten thousand of them. Of women convicted of murder, the overwhelming majority killed their intimate partners or family members, according to a 1999 Department of Justice report.[17] The number of these deaths attributable to self-defense or attempts to escape abuse is unknown because no agency tracks these correlations.

What we do know is largely anecdotal but points to a pattern that official statistics ignore: for women convicted of murder, gendered violence and society's failure to address it often plays a significant, if not causal, role. Take Sissy, for instance. In 2002, Sissy, then forty-eight, was convicted of the murder of her live-in boyfriend. But her story is more complex than that single fear-inducing word lets on. Throughout their eleven-year relationship, her boyfriend, a military veteran, shoved her, hit her, chased her, cut her with a knife, and even pulled a gun on her.

Several times, she ended the relationship and moved out. Each time, he apologized and promised to change. Each time, she believed him and returned to the relationship. That's not unusual. According to domestic violence experts, it typically takes a survivor seven to ten attempts to permanently leave an abusive relationship.

Each time, the arguments and abuse resumed. The abuse escalated when they moved from Virginia, where her family lived, to Alabama, where she knew no one but his family. Still, Sissy was hopeful they could have a loving relationship free of violence.

The couple was in the process of buying a house, which Sissy hoped would stop the violence. One night, she cooked a celebratory dinner. But her boyfriend didn't feel like celebrating; instead, he began arguing with her, then jumped across the coffee table, wrapped his hands around her neck, and began to choke her. When he let go, she grabbed his gun and fled. He chased her down the building corridor.

"I was not trying to shoot him," Sissy explained in a letter from prison, "but the gun just started going off and wouldn't stop. It was like fireworks." She panicked, dropped the gun, and ran. "I never knew that he was in the range of the gunfire. It's like I never saw him, I never knew he got hit. As far as I knew, he was still after me."[18] She later turned herself in. Given the numerous police reports documenting her partner's abuse, the police initially told her that nothing would happen. Several days later, however, she was arrested, Eventually, she was prosecuted, convicted, and sentenced to fifty years in prison. Sissy is now in her sixties and, if forced to serve the entire sentence, will not leave prison until she is ninety-eight years old.

As Sissy's story illustrates, the threat of imprisonment did not prevent her boyfriend's acts of violence and abuse or his death.

But don't we need prisons to protect ourselves from people whose acts are brutal and illogical and not committed in self-defense? That could describe the acts of Sissy's boyfriend (or any abusive partner) who remained undeterred by the threat of arrest or prison.

That could also describe the actions of fifteen-year-old Paula Cooper. In 1985, Cooper was one of four teenagers who decided to rob seventy-seven-year-old Ruth Pelke. They knocked on her door and asked for Bible lessons. Once Pelke invited them inside, the girls beat her, stabbed her thirty-three times, then stole her car and ten dollars. After their arrest, the other three girls pointed to Cooper as their ringleader; she was convicted and sentenced to death, becoming the youngest person on death row in the US.[19]

Pelke's grandson Bill was in the courtroom when Cooper was sentenced to death. So was Cooper's grandfather, who wailed in despair when the death sentence was announced. Despite the man's grief, Bill thought justice had been served.

The following year, however, Pelke realized that his grandmother, a devout Christian, would have wanted him to have compassion for and forgive Cooper—and certainly would not have wanted the teenager executed. That night, Bill, who shared his grandmother's faith, prayed and forgave the girl, resolving to help overturn her death sentence. Her sentence was eventually commuted to sixty years in prison and, in 2013, Cooper, then age forty-three, was released from prison.[20]

The threat of imprisonment—and even execution—did not deter Cooper and her teenage friends from their brutal and illogical actions. Cooper's story also illustrates another point that is often overlooked in conversations about crime and punishment—not every family member or loved one wants retribution. Prosecutors often seize upon a family's grief to push for the most punitive charge and sentence. But during his efforts to overturn Cooper's sentence and the years following her commutation, Pelke met other families who opposed the death penalty for the people who had killed their loved ones.[21] In 1993, Pelke and some of these other family members formed Journey of Hope to advocate an end to the death penalty. Every year, members embark upon a seventeen-day speaking tour across a different state to promote love, compassion, and an end to state-sponsored executions.

The threat of incarceration has also not stopped mass shootings. In June 2015, a twenty-one-year-old white man named Dylann Roof entered a Black church in Charleston, South Carolina, and began shooting. He killed nine people. Roof later told police that he had chosen that church because he wanted to kill Black people.[22]

Police had had contact with Roof twice in the months before he opened fire. In the first instance, he had entered a shopping mall wearing all black and began questioning store employees about how many people worked there and what hours the store was open. His questions unsettled the employees, who called the police. Finding the drug Suboxone on Roof, officers arrested him for misdemeanor drug possession and banned him from the mall for a year. Less than two weeks later, one of the officers involved in the mall questioning saw Roof loitering by his car near a park. The officer searched his car and found a forearm grip for an AR-15 semiautomatic rifle and six unloaded magazines, which were capable of holding forty rounds. Roof told the officer he did not have enough money to buy an AR-15.[23]

Those two instances of police contact did not deter Roof from his intentions. The threat of incarceration did not stop his massacre. Roof later admitted he had saved ammunition to shoot himself after his rampage; he refrained only because he did not see police arriving. The threat of arrest and incarceration motivated him to plan suicide as a way out but did not stop him from senselessly murdering nine strangers.

Again and again, we see that incarceration does not prevent rape or murder. If it did, the US would have the world's lowest rates of sexual assault and murder since it has the highest rate of incarceration. But given the low rates of reporting, investigating, prosecuting, and imprisoning, we see that's not the case. Instead, our reliance on prisons lulls us into ignoring the social, cultural, and economic factors that lead to violence and ultimately make us less safe.

CHAPTER 17

Incarceration and sex offender registries are necessary to keep our children safe.

The systems designed to protect us are actually doing us harm because they disincentivize truth telling and help seeking.

—SUJATHA BALIGA

One in four girls and at least one in six boys is sexually abused before their eighteenth birthday.[1]

Why is that rate so shockingly high? Don't prisons and sex offender registries keep children safe from violence?

That's another myth used to prop up mass incarceration.

Again, we must remember that incarceration doesn't prevent harm; it's a punitive response to harm that has already happened.

Relying on police, prosecutors, and prisons to keep children safe from physical and sexual violence ignores the reality that most of the danger to children comes not from strangers but from people close to them—family members, neighbors, and trusted community members. Ninety-three percent of sexual assaults on children involve family members or acquaintances of the child.[2] But stereotypes that the majority of sexual abuse (of children or adults) comes from "stranger danger" continues to bolster more punitive laws while failing to increase safety.

For Amita Swadhin, the criminal legal system and threat of imprisonment failed to keep her safe from her father's repeated sexual abuse starting from age four. She was not his only target; he also abused Swadhin's mother sexually, verbally, physically, and emotionally. When Swadhin was thirteen, she tried to have him prosecuted. But the prosecutors also threatened to prosecute Swadhin's mother, who had never abused the girl. The threat frightened the teenager into keeping silent about the extent of her father's sexual violence. He ultimately was sentenced to five years of probation.[3]

Swadhin's initial willingness to pursue prosecution (and prosecutors' willingness to take her abuse seriously) is more exceptional than typical. The number of people who are prosecuted and imprisoned for child sexual abuse is even lower than the number who are imprisoned for sexually abusing adults. Only ten to eighteen of every hundred incidents of child sexual abuse are ever reported to authorities. Of those, only six go to trial. Of those six, only three are convicted.[4]

But, notes sujatha baliga, a restorative justice practitioner and director of Impact Justice, those three convictions are not necessarily for child sexual abuse; they are convicted of "something." The maneuverings of the criminal legal system mean that prosecutors often pursue the highest possible charge, a tactic that pressures defendants into pleading guilty to a lesser offense with a lighter sentence. This means that "something" may be a charge far less severe than the abuse actually inflicted.[5]

The overall punitiveness of the criminal legal system and its frequent embrace of mandatory minimum sentences, or lengthy sentences that judges are required to mete out for certain convictions, actually work against child sexual abuse convictions—or any form of acknowledgment, admission, or accountability at all. Lengthy mandatory minimum sentences can cause prosecutors not to file charges or to file charges for a less serious crime. They also increase the number of plea bargains for a less serious (and often not sexual) crime. The threat of long prison sentences encourages people who have committed child sexual abuse to continue to deny any wrongdoing or admit to a lesser charge to avoid the mandatory prison sentence.[6]

Mandatory minimum sentences—and the threat of prison in general—also keep many victims and their family members from reporting the abuse.[7] That's what happened to baliga who, as a child, was deterred from seeking help from her father's sexual abuse by the dual threats of incarceration and deportation. "I had no interest in my father being incarcerated or my mother being deported or in being taken away from my family," she wrote. "Even as a child I knew that if I told anyone what was happening in my home, any of these things could have happened, especially because, for much of my childhood, we were the sole immigrant family in our rural patch of America. This is really important for us to understand, that the systems designed to protect us are actually doing us harm because they disincentivize truth telling and help seeking."[8]

These threats also prevent safety by discouraging abusive people from seeking help. In Maryland, the Johns Hopkins Sexual Disorders Clinic tracked the number of people who voluntarily came forward for treatment for sexually abusive behaviors. The numbers were never high (seven per year or seventy-three over a ten-year period), but when mandatory reporting, or requiring service providers to report suspected child abuse, became law, the number dropped to zero.[9]

Accompanying the threat of incarceration is the vilification of people who harm children as depraved monsters. This portrayal makes it less likely that people will recognize warning signs of sexual abuse from family and community members because they do not see the abusers as "monsters."[10] Instead, people who abuse are also beloved parents, grandparents, and cousins; respected clergy and neighbors; and revered community organizers. The portrayal of people who engage in child sexual abuse as monsters makes it more difficult for survivors to feel their stories will be believed—and for the trusted adults in their lives to do so.

For those who don't plead to lesser charges, incarceration is often accompanied by the sex offender registry, which requires people convicted of certain sexual violence to register even after incarceration. Requirements vary from state to state, but people on the registries generally are prohibited from living near schools, day cares, or other places where children regularly congregate.

Sex offender registries were first enacted in 1990 in Washington State. Other states followed suit, including New Jersey, which passed Megan's Law in 1994 in response to the murder of eight-year-old Megan Kanka who was killed by a man with two previous convictions for sexually assaulting girls. Megan's Law required that information about people with sexual convictions be made public, ostensibly to allow people to protect themselves from those who had committed sexual violence. Two years later, Congress followed suit with a similar national sex offender registration and notification law.

A decade later, in 2007 and 2008, more than 1,500 sex offender–related bills were proposed in legislatures across the country; over 275 of them were enacted into law.[11] Not all registrants have sexually harmed others: at least twenty-nine states require registration for consensual sex between teenagers, at least twelve for public urination, and five for sex work–related offenses.[12] Thirty-eight states place children—some as young as eight years old—on the registry, though less than 3 percent of children who have been adjudicated or convicted of a sex crime go on to do so again.[13] Now more than nine hundred thousand people are on the national registry, a figure higher than the population of Vermont.[14]

But instead of increasing safety for children and families, registries make it more difficult for people with convictions involving children to rebuild their lives after serving their prison sentence.

The Department of Justice found that nationally only 5.3 percent of people convicted of sex offenses were ever rearrested for a new sex offense. In Washington State, researchers found that people who committed sexual harm to children had the lowest sex offense recidivism rates (2.3 percent) of all sex offenders; people who raped adult victims had the highest (3.9 percent).[15]

In New York, researchers examined twenty-one years of arrest data, comparing the decade before and after the state implemented Megan's Law. They found that 95 percent of those arrested for sex offenses had no previous record.[16] In other words, the registry does not give notice or warning to family members of potential child victims; instead, it stigmatizes people and impedes their ability to reintegrate into society.

Though child sexual abuse in the state has declined 64 percent since 1992, convictions for child sex offenses in New York rose 70.8 percent after 1996.[17]

One could argue that prohibiting people with sex offenses from living near children prevents the risk of future violence. But studies have found that these restrictions make very little difference. The Minnesota Department of Corrections tracked the re-offense rate of people who had been imprisoned (and then released) for sex offenses. It found that "not a single re-offense would have been prevented by an ordinance restricting where sex offenders could live."[18]

Texas has among the toughest laws for prosecuting and punishing those accused of crimes against children. That should mean that the children in the Lone Star State are among the safest, but in fact the opposite is the case. Texas has the nation's highest rates of child abuse death (increasing 122 percent from 1997 to 2012), in large part because it provides among the fewest resources to children and families in need.[19]

Not only have incarceration and sex offender registries not correlated with actual instances of child abuse, but they also often work against public safety. Studies have shown that sex offenders who are subject to public notification suffer from significant stress factors, such as the loss of a job or home, harassment, and physical assault. Many are frequently forced to move far away from the support and resources that may keep them stable, which puts them more at risk for re-offense and re-arrest.[20]

In contrast, people with positive support systems, connections to their community, stable housing, and jobs have significantly lower recidivism rates.[21]

Not every survivor wants the most punitive option. One survivor of child sexual abuse recalled consulting a lawyer several years after her abuse.

> I asked him, "What are my options? What should I do?" And he said, "Well that depends. Let's look at what justice looks like for you in response to this situation. Since you are in no danger right now, take time to think. What do you need to happen? Think short term and long term." Grappling with those questions was the most important thing I could do for myself. I think if a different lawyer had presented me with punitive options rather than these questions, I would have just chosen those options without thinking about whether that would make anyone safer or whether that was what I really wanted.[22]

What would those other options look like?

One example is Hollow Water, an Ojibwe reserve north of Winnipeg, Canada. There, two-thirds of Hollow Water's 450 residents have experienced sexual abuse at the hands of family members.

At the same time, Hollow Water residents understood that relying on the traditional criminal legal system required children to testify against their abusive loved ones—and to do so in a way that convinced others that they were telling the truth. It was an approach that fragmented a community that had already been torn apart by decades of residential schools, forced displacement, systemic poverty, and racism.

Realizing that turning people over to the criminal legal system had not stopped the problem in the past, residents decided to try a new approach, one that used restorative justice rather than criminal punishment. "We couldn't just work with the victim. We also had to work with the offender because we felt the offender was the core of the problem," recalled Berma Bushie.[23]

As discussed briefly in chapter 2 and in greater depth in chapter 19, restorative justice is a process that involves not only the person who was harmed and the person who did the harm, but also people who have been indirectly affected, such as family members, neighbors, and community members. They come together to identify and address the harm and also the needs and obligations required to begin the process of healing and accountability.

Most who signed up for the first trainings were women. One of the few men who signed up was Lloyd Bushie, who had also sexually abused others in the past. Through these trainings, Bushie learned how to help address sexual abuse and how to respect women as people. His task became to speak with the people accused of abuse.

Hollow Water residents revived the healing circle, a traditional Native American form of addressing harm and violence. But the Community Holistic Circle Healing was a lengthy process; for one couple, who had sexually abused two of their five children, the process took several years. All of their children had been removed to foster care outside the community; only after the couple had participated in both the healing circle and individual counseling for two years were the children moved to foster care homes within the community. The children began participating in family counseling sessions with their parents. "I could trust my dad being alone with him," stated one of their daughters during a family counseling session. "I couldn't trust him [before]. . . . We sit down and talk about what he done. He keeps telling us over and over how sorry he is. I've come a long way."[24]

There are no programs on the same scope within the United States. In Vermont, a program called Stop It Now! (now defunct) provided support to people who had committed child sexual abuse. The program followed a public health approach similar to campaigns against drunk driving; through both media and public outreach, Stop It Now! provided information on how to recognize and address child sexual abuse. It also provided resources and encouragement to those who were abusive and wanted to change their behavior. At the same time, the state's juvenile justice system sponsored a presentence alternative program for adolescents and children who had perpetrated sexually abusive acts. Between 1995 and 1999, over one hundred people, nearly all adolescents, voluntarily came forward for help with sexually abusive behaviors and acts.[25] Despite these successes, Stop It Now! was only able to continue for another five years before a lack of funding forced its closure in 2004.

Prisons—and the accompanying threat of the sex offender registry—have proven ineffective at keeping children and adults safe from physical or sexual violence. Instead, prisons misdirect our attention away from recognizing and addressing potentially abusive behavior in our communities to fear and panic of monstrous strangers. They also direct our attention away from developing and funding resources that would help family and community members and toward carceral mechanisms that tear families and communities apart.

CHAPTER 18

The system is broken and we simply need some reforms to fix it.

What are the possibilities of non-reformist reform—of changes that, at the end of the day, unravel rather than widen the net of social control through criminalization?

—RUTH WILSON GILMORE

The 2.3 million people in jails, prisons, and immigrant detention centers have stretched government budgets, often at the expense of needed social services such as healthcare, housing, and education.

As the numbers of people in jails, prisons, and other forms of correctional control have grown, so too has public awareness. Advocates, including formerly incarcerated people, have spent decades pointing to the destruction wrought by mass incarceration and its devastating effects on communities of color, but politicians, mainstream media, and the general public ignored their declarations for years.

Now the skyrocketing number of people behind bars, ongoing stories of the brutal and dehumanizing conditions inside, and the amount of money hemorrhaging from state and local budgets to keep people confined have brought the issue of mass incarceration to greater public attention. Some of the most visible and vocal discussions around mass incarceration often revolve around the premise that the system is broken but can be fixed with some tinkering. Incarceration should only be used for the most dangerous people, goes the new wisdom. At the same time, prison conditions need to be fixed so that incarceration can become rehabilitative or restorative, just like the prisons in Norway (described in the following chapter).

But the criminal legal system isn't broken. It's functioning as intended—as a form of surveillance, control, and punishment and as a way to conceal rather than address society's problems.

Why is it important to challenge the idea that the system is broken but, with a few repairs and reforms, can be fixed?

Once upon a time, politicians might have run on electoral platforms of being tough on crime and touting law and order, but their new refrain now advocates using incarceration only for people who are considered dangerous and fixing conditions inside so they can be rehabilitated. If we think about the system as simply needing some reforms, then we might buy into these new tunes.

But if we look at the history that brought us to this moment of mass incarceration and mass criminal control, we'd see that, actually, the system is working as intended—targeting and incapacitating people and communities that are considered undesirable, including Black people and other people of color, immigrants, and people who bucked social norms. As the system expands, it sucks more and more people into its web, including people who were not initially targets, such as white and/or middle-class citizens.

Across the country, advocates and organizations have mounted campaigns for decarceration, or the shrinking of the prison population by releasing more people from prisons while simultaneously fighting for reforms that would prevent people from being imprisoned.

Decarceration efforts address varied aspects of mass incarceration. Some advocates fight for sentencing reform, which would allow people who had previously been sentenced under draconian laws during the 1980s and 1990s to apply for resentencing and a chance at a shorter prison sentence. Others fight for sentencing reforms that would keep people from being sentenced to these lengthy terms in the future. While many of these efforts focus on people imprisoned for nonviolent offenses, some, such as the Corrections-Mitigating Factor law in Illinois and the Domestic Violence Survivors Justice Act in New York, also include those with violent convictions.

In some states, organizers are pushing for laws and policies that will allow people to be released from prison and stop draconian sentences from being meted out in the future. This can take the form of efforts to abolish life without parole (LWOP), in which a person is ineligible to apply for parole no matter how much time has passed or how many rehabilitative efforts they have made. Campaigns to abolish LWOP have been mounted in California and Pennsylvania, largely led by family members of people currently serving LWOP sentences.

Advocates are also addressing the imprisonment of hundreds of people who have already served decades and still have decades left on sentences that were imposed during the 1970s, 1980s, and 1990s as well as the reality that keeping aging people in prison does not increase public safety.

In California, advocacy efforts led to the passage of an elder parole law in 2017. The law, which took effect in January 2018, enables people who are sixty years or older and have served at least twenty-five years of their sentence to be eligible for parole consideration. It did not guarantee that the parole board would grant them parole—only that they would have an opportunity to appear before the board. The bill contained exceptions to parole consideration: people who were sentenced under the state's three-strikes law, those sentenced to life without parole, and those convicted of first-degree murder of a peace officer.

In New York State, the Release Aging People in Prison campaign is organizing to pass a slightly different elder parole bill that would require an immediate parole interview for people who are fifty-five or older and have served at least fifteen years of their sentence.

Other advocates have mounted campaigns for clemency. Clemency can take two forms. One is a commutation, or a shortening, of a person's prison sentence; the other is a pardon, which wipes out a person's conviction. Clemency can be granted to people in state or federal prisons. Some clemency campaigns focus on a single person serving a particularly unjust sentence, while other campaigns push for clemency for a larger group, such as people imprisoned under the war on drugs, survivors of domestic violence, or people sentenced as juveniles.

For the 183,000 people sentenced to federal prison, the president has the power to grant clemency. In 2015, when Obama announced his clemency initiative, advocates, including formerly incarcerated people, seized the moment to mount campaigns drawing attention to people sentenced to lengthy, if not life, sentences under drug war policies. In the end, Obama commuted the sentences of 1,715 people in federal prison, many of whom had been sentenced to lengthy sentences for nonviolent drug offenses. Tens of thousands of others had their hopes dashed when their clemency applications were denied—or simply not acted upon.

The 1.3 million people in state prisons must appeal to their state's governor for clemency. In some states, they have been doing just that. In Ohio, as described in chapter 15, incarcerated abuse survivors launched a mass clemency campaign in the 1990s, resulting in clemency for twenty-five women. In California, organizers pushed outgoing governor Jerry Brown to commute people sentenced to life without parole to sentences that would make them eligible for parole. Before leaving office in 2018, Brown commuted the sentences of 152 people, many of whom had originally been sentenced to life without parole.[1] In New York, organizers with Survived and Punished have mounted clemency campaigns for abuse survivors imprisoned for self-defense. (As of May 2020,

New York's governor, Andrew Cuomo, has granted clemency to only two domestic violence survivors and a total of twenty-one people in prison.[2])

Some of these decarceration efforts dovetail with abolition, or the fight to eliminate prisons altogether. Drawing from the eighteenth- and nineteenth-century movements to abolish slavery, prison abolitionists reject the premise that prisons are broken and simply in need of some reforms to fix them. Instead, they argue, prisons—and mass incarceration—are working as intended—to control people who have been marginalized by society and to hide society's inequities behind walls and barbed wires rather than address them. Meanwhile, as discussed in chapter 3, prisons offer scant resources for reflection and rehabilitation while creating numerous roadblocks to self-transformation efforts. This has led to some criminal justice reformers—and even prison officials—to focus on improving conditions to make prisons more rehabilitative or restorative like the prisons in Norway and other Scandinavian countries (as discussed in chapter 19).

In contrast, abolitionists contend that tearing people away from their families and communities can never be rehabilitative or restorative and that no one belongs in a cage. Thus, rather than reforming prison conditions or advocating reforms that only benefit some portion of people targeted for imprisonment, abolitionists advocate ending incarceration altogether.

Not every person working toward decarceration identifies as an abolitionist. Many people who organize to close jails, end punitive sentencing guidelines, or mount clemency campaigns don't believe that prisons should be entirely eliminated. They may agree with the majority of what abolitionists believe—that mass incarceration, built on a legacy of slavery and genocide, is racist, disproportionately affects people of color and those who are marginalized by society, and that the reliance on prisons usurps resources from addressing societal problems. But they cannot envision a world without prisons.

They're not alone. Many people believe that prisons are necessary for safety and security; they fear abolition would simply open prison gates and push society into a Mad Max type of world. But that's not actually what abolition espouses. Mass incarceration drains resources that could be used instead to address underlying causes of criminalized actions and harm, thus promoting greater safety. Abolition recognizes this and, while calling for dismantling systems of mass incarceration, also advocates investing these newly freed monies and resources into communities and structural supports. Thus, organizing for accessible and affordable housing, accessible (if not universal) medical and mental health care, quality education, access to nutritious foods, and employment that pays living wages fall under abolitionist organizing. All of these campaigns focus on expanding resources that prevent people from being criminalized and funneled into jails and prisons; for those already imprisoned, these campaigns work to meet their needs when they are released.

At the same time, some abolitionists have created initiatives that use restorative justice and transformative justice to address interpersonal harm and violence (which is discussed in greater detail in chapters 20 and 21). They also recognize that organizing for issues that might seem unrelated to incarceration—such as safe and affordable housing, accessible medical and mental health care, quality education, and environmental justice—are part of the same goal: creating a world in which people's needs are met.

Some people involved in prison reform may accuse abolitionists of being unconcerned about the welfare of people who are currently incarcerated and working only toward some distant future in which prisons are eliminated. What about the 2.3 million people currently in jails, prisons, immigrant detention centers, and other forms of confinement?

It's not that people espousing abolition don't care about the welfare of the 2.3 million people currently locked inside. It's that they espouse a vision in which reforms don't lead to a strengthening of the prison system or a widening of the carceral net. That means that abolitionists are unlikely to mount campaigns to build mental health jails or simply modernized jails. This became apparent in the debates around the campaign to close Rikers Island, New York's island jail, which has long been notorious for its entrenched culture of violence. While many criminal justice reform organizations backed a proposal by the mayor and local politicians to build four new jails to replace the crumbling and dilapidated buildings at Rikers, abolitionists organized on a platform of No New Jails, arguing that new jails do not address the underlying causes of criminalization and incarceration. They also noted that the money for building these new jails—over eight billion dollars—would be better spent on resources such as affordable housing, community-based and culturally responsive mental health programs, and education.

The abolitionist stance against the new jails led some reform organizations and advocates to accuse No New Jails organizers of not caring about the nearly eight thousand people currently enduring torturous conditions at Rikers Island.[3] But the reluctance to endorse new jails doesn't mean that abolitionists are unconcerned with the welfare of people currently inside jails. Abolitionists have joined fights to end cash bail, drastically limit or end solitary confinement, eliminate life without parole sentences, and support organizing by people inside jails and prisons. In New York City, for instance, organizers with No New Jails paired their efforts of opposing new jails with writing to and raising money for incarcerated organizers, protesting outside jails that lacked heat during bitterly cold winter weeks, and posting bail for women (trans and cisgender) currently confined at Rikers.

At the same time, abolitionists have also been sharply critical of criminal justice reforms that shift people from brick-and-mortar jails and prisons into other forms of surveillance and control. Many of these efforts not only fail to address the lack of societal resources but also often serve to widen the net, allowing the legal system to exert surveillance and control over more people.

Electronic monitoring is one of these reforms. It has become increasingly popular as an alternative to physical imprisonment, both on the pretrial and post-conviction side. Under electronic monitoring, a person is required to have a global positioning system (GPS) device shackled to their ankle. The device allows the monitoring company to track the person's location at all times. The person may not be behind bars, but their movements are still strictly regulated—each week, they have to submit a list of destinations, including times, for the approval by the authorities (usually the probation officer or the monitoring company, depending on the jurisdiction). Going to work is usually permitted, but stopping at the library to grab some reading material or bring a child to story time probably won't be. Picking up a child from school each day is usually permitted, but attending their basketball games is not.[4] Thanksgiving at Grandma's might be approved, but a cousin's graduation party probably won't be. Even walking the dog on the other side of the street can be prohibited. The electronic monitor allows a person to live at home with their family but prevents them from fully participating in their family's lives.

As of 2016, more than 130,000 people were under electronic monitoring.[5] This includes people who are awaiting trial. Despite not having been found guilty, their lives are still restricted by this alternative to spending their pretrial waiting time in jail. In 2020, as COVID-19 ravaged the nation's largest jails, electronic monitoring became an increasingly attractive alternative to overcrowded jails. In Chicago, for instance, 3,167 people awaiting trial were placed on electronic monitoring instead of jailed, so many that the sheriff's office ran out of devices.[6]

Many people do prefer to be at home with their families rather than locked away in a jail or prison. Sleeping in one's own bed is generally preferable than sleeping on a prison bunk. Eating food out of one's own refrigerator is vastly preferred to the limited (and unhealthy) options offered by prison cafeterias and commissaries. During a public health crisis, being released from cramped cells and crowded dorms can be a lifesaver. But abolitionists, often led by those who have experienced the confines of monitoring, recognize that replacing physical incarceration with electronic incarceration, or e-carceration, doesn't end mass incarceration; it simply shifts it to another form.[7]

When thinking about the system of mass incarceration and efforts to change it, it's useful to consider the question posed by prison scholar and abolitionist Ruth Wilson Gilmore: "What are the possibilities of non-reformist reform—of changes that, at the end of the day, unravel rather than widen the net of social control through criminalization?"[8]

CHAPTER 19

We should make our prisons more like those in Norway.

Treat people like dirt and they will be dirt. Treat them
like human beings and they will act like human beings.

—GOVERNOR OF BASTØY PRISON, Norway

When we talk about rehabilitation in prison—and the failure of US prison systems to offer rehabilitative programming and opportunities, reformers often point to the prison system in Norway.

"Yesterday I visited Rikers Island," said Kim Ekhaugen, the director of Norway's prison system, at a panel discussion in New York City. "The prison population of Norway is four thousand. It would fit into one corner of the island."[1]

Norway and its neighboring Scandinavian countries (Denmark, Finland, and Sweden) follow a social and economic system often referred to as the Nordic model. While each country differs in its approach, each uses a free market capitalist system characterized by an elaborate social safety net, including free education and universal healthcare, strong pension plans, high rates of unionization among workers, and greater gender equity.

These countries are also known for their more humane approaches to incarceration as well as their low incarceration rates. Norway, for instance, incarcerates approximately four thousand of its five million residents. Sentences are short, averaging about eight months compared to three (or more) years in the United States.[2]

Norway initially modeled its prison system after Pennsylvania's penitentiary system. The country's prisons resembled the Eastern State Penitentiary in Philadelphia with high fortress-like walls and single cells where people were confined alone to repent their crimes. But in the 1960s and 1970s, the country shifted from a punitive penal model to one in which incarcerated people were viewed—and treated—like neighbors, family members, and community members who would one day return to society.

Today many of Norway's prisons are considered at the forefront of "normalization" and humaneness. One-third of its incarcerated people are in open prisons where they live in cottages with three to five others. In these prisons, they work, study, shop for groceries, cook their own meals, and receive visitors in a more homelike environment. Living conditions are meant to mirror the outside world, a process known as "normalization," in which incarcerated people are prepared to return to society as neighbors, family members, and community members. They are allowed to vote in national elections and are paid a daily average of 63.50 NOK (or eight US dollars).[3] Officers are trained to treat the people in custody humanely.

Rather than treating incarcerated people as disposable to society, Norway's approach to incarceration is based on an understanding that people are sent to prison as punishment. The loss of freedom and separation from their families and communities is the punishment; they are not sent to prison to suffer additional forms of punishment. Norway's approach is also based on the understanding that incarcerated people will return to society. As the governor (Norway's term for the warden or superintendent) of Bastøy, one of the country's open prisons, summed up, "Treat people like dirt and they will be dirt. Treat them like human beings and they will act like human beings."[4]

The Nordic model has garnered international praise. Prison administrators from across the United States have visited Norway's prison system and brought some of its reforms back to their state prisons. North Dakota, for instance, revamped its system of solitary confinement. The Oregon prison system exchanged correctional officers with Norway, sending some of its prison staff to live and work with correctional officers in Norway and inviting Norwegian prison staff to conduct trainings in the state's fourteen prisons.[5] The new Colorado prisons director wants to revamp the state's entire prison system to resemble Norway's.[6]

But there are some darker aspects to this seemingly glowing prison system. Women make up approximately 6 percent of the country's prison population, or 202 women as of 2018.[7] But these 202 women don't always benefit from the same normalization efforts and rehabilitative opportunities extended to their male counterparts.

Of those 202 women, approximately 70 are confined in Bredtveit, Norway's open prison for women; open prisons have a more home-like environment and fewer restrictions on movement than other prisons. Many more women, however, are excluded from this nicer, normalized prison. Instead, they are double-bunked, or share cells originally built for one person, within prisons that are often old and dilapidated. Some cells in these non-open prisons lack toilets. Additionally, some prisons do not allow women out of their cells at night to use the toilet, a condition that the government ombudsman sharply criticized.[8] In these prisons, they are unable to access the rehabilitative opportunities or even comparable outdoor recreation space and physical activity offered to their male counterparts.[9]

Director Kim Ekhaugen blamed the disparate treatment on the relatively small number of women who are incarcerated—and thus neglected in the normalization efforts. But that same year, he also noted, Norway imprisoned eight youths who were between the ages of fifteen and eighteen. Rather than dismissing them as an insignificant fraction of the country's prison population, penal authorities poured more resources into ensuring their rehabilitation and opportunities for reintegration into society. Norway has two juvenile units, each of which incarcerates four young people; each unit has nineteen staff members who work with these four youths.[10]

Not everyone is happy with the country's humane penal system. A 2010 survey found that 80 percent of Norwegians felt that punishment was too lenient. There's also a growing dissatisfaction, rooted in racism and xenophobia among an otherwise homogenous population, with the prison conditions under which noncitizens are confined. In 2011, Per Sandberg, the leader of the country's Progress Party, proclaimed that "foreign criminals are a big problem and mild sentences and high-quality facilities aren't helping." Sandberg proposed a ten-point plan to make prison conditions more austere: incarcerated Norwegians would have their prison wages halved while non-Norwegians would not receive any wages at all. Non-Norwegians would be placed in prisons with lower standards than their citizen counterparts.[11]

A few months later, Ullersmo Prison in the eastern part of the country created a segregated cell block specifically for foreign nationals. One year later, in 2012, the government announced that Kongsvinger, a ninety-seven-bed prison in eastern Norway, would be converted into a segregated prison for foreign nationals who would be deported after completing their prison sentences. Surprisingly, the change did not result in a decline in conditions. The prison provided the same healthcare as it did for incarcerated citizens in other prisons. While the education department was mandated to stop teaching the incarcerated noncitizens skills that would give them "further ties to Norwegian society," they did not cease programming. Instead, they shifted their focus from teaching Norwegian to teaching English; they stopped teaching about the Norwegian building code but continued to teach building construction.[12]

The country's relatively small prison population is in part because Norway has a waiting list to enter prisons. While prison sentences are generally short (three months is a typical sentence), prison construction has still failed to keep pace with the growing number of people sentenced to prisons by the court. In 2014, approximately 1,300 people were waiting to enter prison and begin their sentences; some prisons began housing two people in cells that were formerly single occupancy.[13]

To address these growing numbers, the country's minister of justice attempted to lease unused space in a Swedish prison in 2013. When the Swedish government refused, he sought assistance from the Netherlands, which agreed. By October 2014, the Dutch-Norwegian prison confined 153 people; 80 percent were foreign nationals from Norway. The distance made visits from friends and family much more difficult, if not impossible, but that became a less pressing issue given that most of the prison's inhabitants would be subject to deportation upon release from prison and thus were not viewed as part of Norway's society.[14]

Norway's prison population of roughly four thousand also excludes those held in immigrant detention, a population that has been rising in recent years. Many are held in Trandum, an immigration detention center, which has been the site of fires, attempted escapes, and small-scale riots. But, again, because those in immigrant detention are subject to deportation, they are not seen as future neighbors and community members and are excluded from the rehabilitation and reentry initiatives that characterize Norway's much-lauded humane approach to incarceration.

Norway is also embracing electronic monitoring, or "tagging." Under electronic monitoring, a person is shackled to a monitoring device that tracks their every movement, which must be preapproved by penal authorities. In the United States, more than 130,000 people are under electronic monitoring; deviation from the preapproved itinerary can result in jail or prison time.[15] In Norway, 95 people served their entire sentence on electronic monitoring in 2008. By 2013, that number had increased to 1,681.[16] It remains unclear whether the growth of tagging is replacing incarceration for lower level offenses or if, as in the United States, it is widening the penal net for actions that might not otherwise result in some form of state control.

Rehabilitative methods have not worked for everyone. In 2011, Anders Breivik, a far-right Norwegian citizen, set off a car bomb outside the office of the prime minister before opening fire and killing seventy-seven people, many of them teenagers attending a leftist summer camp. He was sentenced to twenty-one years in prison, a sentence that many in the United States found shockingly lenient. But in Norway, where the average prison sentence is three months, his sentence was the maximum that could be imposed under the country's penal code. Breivik was held in isolation away from other incarcerated people. That would not be unusual in a US prison, where approximately eighty thousand people are held in some form of solitary confinement. But solitary in Norway means that Breivik was held in a three-cell suite where he had video games, a DVD player, a typewriter, books, newspapers, and exercise equipment.[17] He is also allowed to take correspondence courses from the University of Oslo. But none of these accommodations seem to have changed Breivik's racist worldview: in court, before arguing that these conditions were inhumane, Breivik threw a Nazi salute to the court and attendees.[18]

But Norway has a built-in safeguard, one that is much less discussed in conversations extolling its prison system. The Norwegian system can employ "preventive detention," or a mechanism in which prison administrators can petition courts to extend a person's incarceration if they believe that person still poses a danger to society. That is what Ekhaugen has stated he will do when Breivik's twenty-one-year prison sentence is up.

Breivik is not the only person to have experienced solitary confinement in Norway's much-praised prisons. Even in the open prisons, people are expected to show up for the morning "body count," in which officers count them to ensure no one has escaped. During that time, officers collect urine samples to test for drug use; those who refuse or fail to produce a urine sample are placed in a solitary cell with a pitcher of water for several hours. These cells are called "solar cells" (*solcelle*) because, on sunny days, the sunlight beats through the windows; in the prison handbook, they are referred to as "leisure single rooms" (*fritidsenerom*) though no one inside the prison uses that term.[19]

Ekhaugen also noted that people with mental illnesses are placed repeatedly in solitary confinement, in large part because, while prisons hire outside mental health providers to work with its prisoners, they still lack the capacity to address severe or chronic mental health issues. Outside of prison, the country also lacks adequate mental health resources, turning its prisons into the de facto depository for those with mental illness.

Norway's incarceration is also expensive. Ekhaugen notes that the Halden Prison, Norway's prime example of a humanitarian maximum-security prison, cost $250 million to build. The yearly spending comes out to $93,000 per person. For 251 incarcerated men, that's an annual expense of $23,343,000. (In comparison, US prisons spend an average of $31,000 per year to incarcerate a single person.)[20] "We will never build another prison like that because it is so expensive," Ekhaugen admitted.[21]

Yes, the US should follow Norway's example of treating incarcerated people not as garbage to be disposed of but as people who are family and community members who will eventually return to society. At the same time, instead of simply pointing to Norway's prison system as the shining beacon for all prisons, we should take note of the social, economic, and political conditions in Norway that are lacking in the United States: its commitment to public services for all of its citizens, including free education, universal healthcare, protection of workers' rights, greater gender equality, and its understanding that people behind bars are still members of families, communities, and society.

CHAPTER 20

Prisons are the only logical and evident way to address violent crime and meet the needs of victims.

Restorative justice is a process that centers on the victim and their needs, not only allowing them to have a voice in the proceedings but also addressing their needs.

P eople often assume that imprisonment meets the needs of victims, an assumption that has been disproven repeatedly by people who have been harmed by violence. So whose needs are met—and whose are ignored? And who decides what their needs are?

Young Black men are more likely to be robbed or victimized by violence, including homicide, than other demographics.[1] They're also the least likely to be considered victims by police, prosecutors, and others in the judicial system. They are frequently unable to access the help and resources they need to address their trauma and begin to heal.[2] Instead, they are often viewed as criminals and disproportionately targeted by the criminal legal system through racist policing practices, overzealous prosecutors, and jurors who see them only as perpetrators of harm.

Young Black men are not the only victims failed by the criminal legal system and its ever-present threat of incarceration. As noted in chapter 17, over three-quarters (or 770 of every 1,000) of sexual assaults go unreported to law enforcement. Of the 230 that are reported, only 46 lead to arrest. Of those 46, only 9 are referred to prosecutors and 5 lead to a conviction. As noted in chapter 18, of every one hundred incidents of child sexual abuse, fewer than twenty are reported; only six go to trial and only three are convicted.

Meanwhile, the survivor is compelled to tell her experience again and again—first to the police, then to the prosecutor, and then again on the witness stand where the adversarial nature of the court system means that every detail will be scrutinized and challenged by the defense attorney. If the person who committed the sexual assault is convicted, the survivor has no say in the sentence.

Having no say in the sentence is true in all court cases involving violence, as DeVitta Briscoe experienced firsthand. In 2010, her seventeen-year-old son was fatally shot by another seventeen-year-old; the shooting was an accident. Prosecutors sought the highest possible sentence, plus a sentencing enhancement (or additional time) for illegal possession of a gun. It was a sentence that Briscoe never wanted and, had her wishes actually been considered, would have argued against.

But Briscoe was never notified of the sentencing hearing, where she could have stated her wishes for leniency and mercy.[3] "I was tossed aside and never heard from the prosecutor again," she said.[4] The court process, she learned, had nothing to do with helping victims and survivors heal; instead, it was about seeking the maximum punishment.

Washington State, where Briscoe lives, is one of fourteen states that does not offer parole. But in thirty-six other states, people in prison typically become eligible for parole after serving a certain number of years behind bars. In some states, this means they appear before a parole board, which typically consists of two or three commissioners appointed by the governor. In other states, the person seeking parole does not appear in person but simply submits a mountain of paperwork demonstrating their efforts at rehabilitation while in prison.

In either scenario, parole commissioners weigh any opposition from the survivor. This means that years after the attack, the survivor must write a letter opposing parole—and often relive the violence and trauma of their experience. Not every victim or survivor writes a letter opposing parole; many do not. But the letters that are written reflect the ways in which incarceration has not aided in the survivor's healing and recovery. Incarceration may grant them temporary peace of mind in removing the person who harmed them, but if incarceration actually addressed the needs of survivors, then their letters would reflect that. Instead, they reveal the same pain and anguish years, and sometimes decades, later.

That's because incarceration is not equipped or designed to address the needs of survivors. It is designed to incapacitate people and remove them from their homes, families, and communities. The needs of survivors—including counseling, medical care, mental health care, safer housing, safer neighborhoods, or safer relationships—are not taken into consideration.

If incarceration doesn't work to address the needs of victims—while also holding the perpetrators of harm accountable—what might work instead?

One solution, which is gaining more attention, is restorative justice. Restorative justice is a process that centers on the victim and their needs, not only allowing them to have a voice in the proceedings but also addressing the needs that they have. Restorative justice involves both the survivor and the person who caused the harm; it also includes people who have been indirectly affected by the experience, such as loved ones, neighbors, and community members. The process often involves a facilitated meeting or peace circle, in which each person who has been affected, either directly or indirectly, shares how the experience has impacted them. Survivors have the opportunity to talk about how they have been harmed—and the lasting consequences of that harm—and to identify their needs. In many cases, those needs include ensuring that no one else goes through what they did—and what they need the person who caused the harm to do in order to ensure that.

Restorative justice as a way to address harm and violence is not new. Today's processes have been adapted from approaches like the peacemaking circles of the Navajo and other Native communities in North America and Maori practices in New Zealand.

In the United States, some jurisdictions are starting to turn to restorative justice as an alternative to the traditional criminal court process with its threat of imprisonment. Common Justice, founded in 2008, is one such program for sixteen-to-twenty-four-year-olds facing violent felony charges in New York City's court system. Both the prosecutor and the victims must agree that the case can be referred to Common Justice instead of the typical court process. Then follows months of preparation on both sides—the person who was harmed and the person responsible for their trauma—until they are ready to come together in a dialogue and talk about what happened and the lasting effects of that experience. Through that dialogue, the two reach agreements about what the person who committed the harm can do to make amends. If that person fulfills those agreements and continues to participate in Common Justice's violence intervention curriculum for the following year, the felony charges are dismissed. The program also continues to work with the survivors to help heal from the violence.[5]

When Common Justice approaches survivors of violence, 90 percent choose to engage in restorative justice rather than the traditional criminal court proceedings. That might seem astounding, but their willingness to participate might be based more on pragmatism than benevolence: more than 90 percent of cases (94 percent at the state level and 97 percent at the federal level) result in plea bargains, meaning that the person accused of a crime pleads guilty to a lesser charge rather than take their chances at trial where they face the maximum possible prison sentence if found guilty.[6] "Survivors know the system cannot be trusted to validate their suffering, give them answers or even a meaningful opportunity to be heard. Nor can it be trusted to keep them or others safe," reflected Michelle Alexander, author of *The New Jim Crow*.[7]

Alameda County in California adopted a restorative justice program for juveniles in 2010. Like Common Justice, the program relies on the cooperation of the district attorney and the victim. If both agree, the young person who is accused of a crime goes through the program and takes responsibility for the harm he or she has caused. The process culminates in a meeting between the victim and the person causing the harm in which he or she apologizes and agrees to make amends. These amends might include paying the victim back, performing community service, or going through an anger management program. If the person fulfills all of the requirements, including making amends, the charges are dropped.

Within the first two years, 102 youths were diverted from the criminal legal system into the program. Those who took part were 44 percent less likely to commit another crime within twelve months of completing the program.[8] In addition, 91 percent of the victims who participated said they would participate in another restorative justice program rather than go through the traditional criminal legal channels, and an equal number (91 percent) said that they would recommend the process to a friend.[9]

As of 2016, thirty-five states had adopted laws that encourage restorative justice either before or after imprisonment.[10]

Restorative justice has also been implemented for violence on much larger scales. Rwanda, for instance, employed a precolonial form of participatory justice to address perpetrators of its 1994 genocide.

Between April and June 1994 Hutu militia and soldiers slaughtered some eight hundred thousand Tutsis and Hutus who were politically moderate or attempted to assist the Tutsis. After the genocide, the Hutu perpetrators were placed in any available prison space, resulting in 130,000 people crammed into prisons with a capacity of 12,000 as they awaited their trials.[11] Trying nearly 100,000 people charged with genocide would have taken between 150 and 200 years.

Instead of using the justice system Rwanda had in place, the country turned to the gacaca court system, a precolonial form of Rwandan justice that had been used to settle local disputes before the Germans introduced incarceration into the country's justice system.

In 2005, the president ordered a mass release of twenty-two thousand people awaiting trial for genocide. But they were not free to simply resume their lives; instead, they still had to answer for their crimes through gacaca. Gacaca, which literally translates to "grass" and, in this context, has been used to mean "justice among the grass," are the community courts aimed at establishing the truth of what had happened and begin the process of reconciliation and forgiveness.

In its precolonial form, gacaca typically resulted in plans for restitution, which could take the form of material payments, beatings, or death. In the twenty-first century, however, gacaca justice took the form of being sentenced to one of about forty *travaux d'intérêt général* (TIG, or "works of general service") camps. In those camps, reparations took the form of labor—building roads, schools, and houses for the homeless, including those who survived the genocide.

On the surface, TIG camps might sound similar to the convict labor and convict leasing that replaced slavery after the Civil War in the United States. But what makes these TIG camps different is that those sentenced to the camps work only part of the week. Some are able to live at home and commute to their labor assignments. They are also educated in not only construction skills but also civic education, literacy, Rwandan history, and government policy.

Between 2006 and 2012, approximately twelve thousand gacacas tried over 1.2 million cases.[12] However, the process hasn't been perfect. Human rights groups raised concerns about the lack of legal representation for the accused person and the qualifications of the locally elected judges, who preside over the gacaca.[13] Sometimes those accused of participating in the genocide admitted to being part of a blockade or group that killed Tutsi people, but they refused to admit personal culpability. Seven years after the last ga-caca, over 149,000 people sentenced by the gacaca had yet to fulfill their requirements.[14]

Imperfect as it is, the process has helped family members fi-nally learn the fate of their loved ones and, in many cases, locate their bodies so they could be properly buried.

Restorative justice is not a perfect process. As the gacaca in Rwanda demonstrate, restorative justice can help bring closure and a start to reconciliation. But the process also depends on the willingness of those who caused the harm to take responsibility for their acts and understand how they have caused harm. At the same time, we must remember that incarceration often fails to hold perpetrators accountable for the harm they've caused—and the adversarial nature of the criminal court system, combined with the threat of imprisonment, often causes people to deny any wrongdoing or responsibility. That denial follows them into the prison system, where little, if anything, encourages them to re-flect on the harm they've caused and what they can do to make amends. In 2015, sixty women came forward with allegations that actor Bill Cosby had drugged and raped them. Cosby was convicted of drugging and sexually assaulting one of those women, Andrea Costand, and he was sentenced to three to ten years in prison. Imprisonment did not spur the actor to reflect upon his actions; instead, in 2020, Cosby, well known for championing personal re-sponsibility, to appeal his conviction, argued, in part, that he was a victim of systemic racism.[15]

Research in the United States, Australia, Canada, and the United Kingdom has demonstrated that restorative justice can help break the cycle of violence and reduce recidivism rates by as much as 44 percent.[16] A study by the University of Pennsylvania found that victims of robbery, assault, and burglary who took part in restorative justice programs reported 37 percent fewer symp-toms of post-traumatic stress than victims who participated in standard court processes.[17] Danielle Sered, founder and director of the restorative justice program Common Justice, said this was partially because these processes "include precisely the things survivors want and don't get from the criminal justice process: answers, voices, control, repair and a belief that others will be protected from the harm they survived." Instead of feeling attacked, those responsible for causing harm "are asked to answer for what they have done from a position that affirms and reorients their personal power, rather than one that aims to constrict it."[18]

The myth of incarceration as the only way to meet the needs of victims ignores the reality that certain victims are less likely to be served and more likely to be criminalized by the legal system. The myth also hides the reality that prisons do little to help the survivor heal. Instead, by locking up the person who caused harm, it freezes both parties into their roles as victim and perpetrator with little or no opportunity for healing or reparations.

CHAPTER 21

Even if societal and political conditions are to blame, there's nothing we can do about it.

How can we respond to violence in ways that not only address the current incident of violence, but also help to transform the conditions that allowed for it to happen?

—MIA MINGUS

Transformative justice uses the power unleashed by the harm of the crime to let those most affected find truly creative, healing solutions.

—RUTH MORRIS

The US reliance on mass incarceration places the onus for crime and violence on the individual, diverting attention from the social, political, and economic conditions that can foster harmful actions. In the traditional courtroom setting, a person can bring up the conditions that have shaped their lives either as a defense or as a plea for a less punitive sentence. If the charge does not require a mandatory minimum sentence, a judge may decide to consider these conditions when meting out a prison sentence.

Ultimately, however, whether the sentence is lenient or harsh and whether it involves jail or prison time or an alternative, a criminal legal sentence does not involve transforming the underlying conditions.

Transformative justice examines the individual and community experiences as well as the social conditions. Unlike the traditional criminal legal system, transformative justice attempts to integrate both personal accountability and social changes.[1] Unlike the original idea of the US penitentiary, in which people were expected to reflect upon and repent their wrongdoings and shortcomings in isolation, transformative justice involves the community—family members, friends, neighbors, coworkers, and others.

Transformative justice differs from restorative justice in that the aim is not just to address the needs and obligations required to begin the healing process but also to transform the conditions that generated or enabled the harm. But the two forms of justice have similar elements, including working with both the person who committed the harm and the person (or people) who were harmed.

Like restorative justice, transformative justice interventions often involve helping survivors access resources that foster healing and safety; working with the harm doer to take responsibility for the harm they've caused; building the capacity of other community members so they can support the intervention, heal, and take responsibility for any harm they were complicit in; and building skills among community members to prevent and interrupt violence.[2]

Transformative justice involves acknowledging that an individual's harmful actions are rooted in social, political, and economic conditions, such as poverty, trauma, isolation, racism, misogyny, homophobia, and/or transphobia, while also recognizing that police, prisons, and other punitive state systems, such as ICE, condone and perpetuate violence.

Mia Mingus, cofounder of the Bay Area Transformative Justice Collective, which builds and supports transformative justice responses to child sexual abuse, defines transformative justice with the following question: How can we respond to violence in ways that not only address the current incident of violence, but also help to transform the conditions that allowed for it to happen?[3]

Unlike the traditional criminal legal system, transformative justice does not have one set approach. Every community engages in transformative justice differently. Furthermore, the approach is often tailored to the harmful actions and the individuals involved. At the same time, notes Mariame Kaba, a transformative justice practitioner and longtime prison abolitionist, "You can't force somebody into being accountable for things they do. . . . People have to take accountability for things that they actually do wrong. They have to decide that this is wrong. They have to say, 'This is wrong and I want to be part of making some sort of amends or repairing this or not doing it again.'"[4]

This means that practitioners do not use transformative justice as an alternative to state intervention; instead, they see it as an approach that gives the harm doer the time and space to take responsibility for their actions.

That's more than what the current criminal legal system encourages. In the court system, defendants are discouraged from admitting harm, let alone taking steps to atone for their behavior. Instead, the court's adversarial system and threat of harsh punishment encourage defendants to deny and minimize any wrongdoing, thus stymieing any exploration of underlying causes or attempts to change them.

Many transformative justice approaches involve a process of community accountability, in which community members work directly with the person who caused the harm to understand the impact of their actions, make amends, take action to repair the damage, and work to change their behavior so they do not repeat this harm. They also work with the person who was harmed to ensure that person has a voice in the process and that their needs are addressed.

There is no cookie-cutter model for community accountability. But there are examples that people can draw from. One such example happened in Seattle when people in the city's punk community decided to take action to address the behavior of Lou, a man employed by a popular club, where he encouraged women to get drunk and then sexually assaulted them.

One of the survivors and her friends confronted Lou in person about the assault. At first, Lou was apologetic but later began justifying and continuing his actions. Frustrated with both his lack of accountability and the sexual violence within the music community, other community members of various genders began to meet and discuss the situation. They also connected with anti-violence organization Communities Against Rape and Abuse (CARA) for support and guidance.

The group's conversations not only centered the survivors' experience but also examined how the person's subculture supported abusive behavior. For instance, the group noted that the popular weekly alternative paper glamorized massive amounts of drinking at Lou's parties. CARA members also identified the community's lack of awareness about sexual violence. With the survivors' consent, the group designed fliers that identified Lou and his behaviors, called for accountability, criticized the local paper, and suggested boycotting the club.

The initial response was discouraging. The newspaper published an article defending Lou and implying that since the survivors had not filed criminal charges, their allegations were not credible. Lou himself threatened to sue them for libel.

But the group persisted, working with survivors to create a document that shared their experiences and provided a critical analysis of the sexual violence and the conditions that enabled it within their community. The group members also defined and called for community accountability. They released the document to the press and posted it online, sparking conversations among members of the community about sexual violence and accountability. As a result, Lou stopped being invited to parties and events, locals began boycotting the club, and out-of-town bands avoided playing there. These consequences prompted Lou to agree to engage with the group through a series of emails, though he ultimately did not take responsibility for his actions.

As email exchanges with Lou became more frustrating and exhausting, group members decided to shift tactics to focus more on community building, education, and prevention. Group members began a process to learn more about sexual violence, safety, and accountability. They learned to facilitate their own safety and accountability workshops. They organized fundraisers for CARA and other anti-violence organizations, raising greater awareness of these groups to members in their community.

As the above example illustrates, community accountability may never reach a happily-ever-after ending. But it's important to note that, while the criminal legal system promises that happily-ever-after, imprisonment rarely delivers it. At the same time, the group's actions opened more conversations and awareness about sexual violence, consent, and prevention, conversations that hopefully shifted the conditions that had enabled Lou's sexual assaults.

"It's a critical shift to decide to use your resources to build the community you want rather than expend all of your resources by fighting the problem you want to eliminate," CARA organizers reflected.[5]

Long-standing reliance on police and prisons has dulled our capacity and willingness to intervene in instances of violence. Understanding this, anti-violence organizers have developed resources to help sharpen that capacity. Creative Interventions, an organization dedicated to providing "resources for everyday people to end violence," developed a 608-page online guide of strategies to stop interpersonal violence.[6] Abuse survivors and organizers Ching-In Chen, Jai Dulani, and Leah Lakshmi Piepzna-Samarasinha compiled an 111-page zine and later a book titled *The Revolution Starts at Home* to document the ways in which organizers have addressed abuse in their circles and communities.[7] Prison abolitionists and transformative justice practitioners Mariame Kaba and Shira Hassan created *Fumbling Towards Repair: A Workbook for Community Accountability Facilitators* for people who are coordinating and facilitating formal community accountability processes.[8]

Across the country, various groups have also created spaces where people can develop and practice responsive intervention skills. At DePaul University in Chicago, for example, students, staff, and faculty work with community organizations to offer skillbuilding workshops through a project called Building Communities, Ending Violence. In these workshops, facilitators use stories of street harassment, dating violence, family violence, sexual or racial harassment, or instances of homophobia and transphobia to encourage participants to brainstorm, imagine, strategize, and role-play collective interventions. After each session, the participants discuss their feelings about the role-play, the strengths and weaknesses of their intervention, and what they learned in the process.[9]

"The goal of the strategy sessions is not to come up with a perfect intervention," explained Ann Russo, one of the project's creators. "Instead, it is to practice what interventions might look like and to reflect on the difficulties, risks, and possibilities that might arise for all involved."[10]

In 2019, organizers created a similar space called the New York City Transformative Justice Hub. Meeting every two months, Hub organizers intended to provide political education about transformative justice and community accountability, a physical space for people to actively engage in the process, consultations and support, and more visibility and connectivity for groups already doing this work.[11]

Another part of transformative justice involves changing the conditions that allow harm and violence to flourish by challenging and dismantling long-held beliefs. In 2005, for instance, the Parliament of India passed the Protection of Women from Domestic Violence Act, which formally recognized and defined domestic violence and allowed courts to impose orders of protection. But domestic and sexual violence continues throughout the country.

In 2008, women who worked with global human rights organization Breakthrough created the Bell Bajao (Hindi for "ring the bell") campaign to encourage men to become more active in addressing the violence within their families and communities.

They created short public service announcement (PSA) videos demonstrating a simple intervention that men could take, an act as simple as ringing the doorbell when they heard or witnessed another man abusing a woman. One video showed a group of young men playing a game of cricket and another showed a neighbor working on his car—the young men and the neighbor both stopping their activity to ring the doorbell to interrupt incidents of domestic violence. These PSAs appeared on television, on the radio, and in print. In addition, mobile vans broadcast the videos, and campaign organizers used these vans to engage neighborhood youth through games, puppet shows, street theater, and quizzes.[12]

The Bell Bajao campaign not only encouraged men to intervene against gender violence but also began changing community attitudes around domestic violence. The campaign seems to have succeeded in changing attitudes and behaviors; one man from the northern state of Uttar Pradesh stated that before he encountered the Bell Bajao campaign, he failed to notice the violence faced by one of his domestic helpers, whose husband beat her and stole her wages. After seeing the campaign, he called the abusive husband, informed him about India's Protection of Women from Domestic Violence Act and told him that if he continued to abuse his wife, he would take action against him. The beatings stopped.[13]

While this intervention stopped the violence, it also engendered a shift—not only in this particular man's awareness of domestic violence but also in his understanding that he, as a man, had the power to intervene and stop ongoing violence. At the same time, he began sharing information about domestic violence—as well as simple acts that could be taken to intervene—with his family and friends.

Bell Bajao is one example of transforming conditions that enable and perpetuate harm. The campaign encourages men to intervene in acts of violence and also helps change society's long-held beliefs about gendered violence and an individual's ability to take action.

The reliance on incarceration diverts attention away from the political, economic, and cultural conditions that generate violence. At the same time, it also deceives people into believing that any attempt to prevent harmful actions or to change the root causes is futile.

Transformative justice is not a substitute for imprisonment. But it is a way to address harm and the conditions that foster and continue to enable harm and violence. As Ruth Morris, the Canadian Quaker who coined the term "transformative justice" explained, "Transformative justice uses the power unleashed by the harm of the crime to let those most affected find truly creative, healing solutions."[14]

For Further Reading

BOOKS

Chen, Ching-In, Jai Dulani, and Leah Lakshmi Piepzna-Samarasinha. *The Revolution Starts at Home: Confronting Intimate Violence within Activist Communities*. Oakland, CA: AK Press, 2016.

Davis, Angela. *Are Prisons Obsolete?* New York: Seven Stories Press, 2003.

Dixon, Ejeris, and Leah Lakshmi Piepzna-Samarasinha. *Beyond Survival: Strategies and Stories from the Transformative Justice Movement*. Oakland, CA: AK Press, 2020.

Gilmore, Ruth Wilson. *Golden Gulag: Prisons, Surplus, Crisis, and Opposition in Globalizing California*. Berkeley: University of California Press, 2006.

Hernández, César Cuauhtémoc García. *Migrating to Prison: America's Obsession with Locking Up Immigrants*. New York: New Press, 2019.

Kim, Alice, Erica Meiners, Audrey Petty, Jill Petty, Beth E. Richie, and Sarah Ross, eds. *The Long Term: Resisting Life Sentences, Working Towards Freedom*. Chicago: Haymarket Books, 2018.

Law, Victoria. *Resistance Behind Bars: The Struggles of Incarcerated Women*. Oakland, CA: PM Press, 2012.

Levine, Judith, and Erica R. Meiners. *The Feminist and the Sex Offender: Confronting Harm, Ending State Violence*. New York: Verso Books, 2020.

Rafter, Nicole Hahn. *Partial Justice: Women, Prisons and Social Control*. New Brunswick, NJ: Transaction Publishers, 1990.

Richie, Beth. *Arrested Justice: Black Women, Violence, and America's Prison Nation*. New York: New York University Press, 2012.

Ross, Rupert. *Returning to the Teachings: Exploring Aboriginal Justice*. Toronto: Penguin Books Canada, 1996.

Russo, Ann. *Feminist Accountability: Disrupting Violence and Transforming Power*. New York: New York University Press, 2019.

Schenwar, Maya. *Locked Down, Locked Out: Why Prisons Don't Work and How We Can Do Better*. San Francisco: Berrett-Koehler Publishers, 2014.

Schenwar, Maya, and Victoria Law. *Prison by Any Other Name*. New York: New Press, 2020.

Simmons, Aishah Shahidah, ed. *Love with Accountability*. Oakland, CA: AK Press, 2019.

Stanley, Eric A., and Nat Smith, eds. *Captive Genders: Trans Embodiment and the Prison Industrial Complex.* Oakland, CA: AK Press, 2011.

Venters, Homer. *Life and Death in Rikers Island.* Baltimore: Johns Hopkins University Press, 2019.

PERIODICALS AND ONLINE RESOURCES

Creative Interventions offers information to help create collective responses to interpersonal harm: http://www.creative-interventions.org.

#8toAbolition: Created in the wake of the 2020 police murder of George Floyd and the international protests that ensued, #8toAbolition compiles a list of abolitionist demands that organizers can use when pressing city and municipal officials: 8toabolition.com.

The Fire Inside: Newsletter of the California Coalition for Women Prisoners. Available online at https://womenprisoners.org.

Interrupting Criminalization is an initiative that aims to interrupt the criminalization and incarceration of women and LGBTQ people of color. Its website includes a tool kit of concrete steps to defund police and invest in community safety: https://www.interruptingcriminalization.com.

Prison Legal News. Select articles available online at https://www.prisonlegal news.org.

The Revolution Starts at Home (original zine). Available online at http://critical resistance.org/wp-content/uploads/2014/05/Revolution-starts-at-home -zine.pdf.

Transform Harm: A website dedicated to transformative justice. It includes an introductory explanation about transformative justice as well as articles, audiovisual resources, and curricula: https://transformharm.org.

Acknowledgments

Books are not written in isolation. Like babies, they require a community to nurture into maturity. This book emerges as a result of countless conversations, meetings, workshops, gatherings and conferences, interviews, and readings.

I'm very grateful to my community for helping me bring this book into the world.

First, many thanks and much appreciation to Steven Englander for his never-ending support and patience: for listening to my endless thinking aloud and letting me vent when I felt stymied. Many men might balk at being left to solo parent for two weeks while their partners travel around the country, but he has always encouraged me to grab every opportunity, whether delivering a keynote speech on women's transatlantic prison resistance at Oxford University or book touring around the Midwest.

Giant hugs to Siuloong Englander, who has been on this journey of thinking and writing about prisons for her entire life. She has visited prisons both in utero and as a rambunctious toddler. She has cheered and cried her way through many conferences (as well as many of her mother's presentations). Until she hit her teenage years, she accompanied me on a number of events during my Never Ending Book Tour (which will be entering Year 12 by the time this hits shelves); her presence ensured that we also took time to explore whatever city we found ourselves in and ate the most delicious vegan food we could find. As I was drafting this book, she whipped up multitudes of vegan dishes that ended up fueling many of my afternoon, evening, and late-night writing sessions.

Jeanne Theoharis was my professor at Brooklyn College years ago. She was the person who set me on the path of finding out what resistance and organizing looked like inside women's prisons, a path that led me to writing my first book and embarking on a reporting beat about incarceration, gender, and resistance. She has never stopped encouraging me—whether as a new mother uncertain about taking on such a daunting research project or as an empty-nesting parent. She also introduced me to Gayatri Patnaik at Beacon; without her, this book may never have emerged. Without her continual encouragement, I'm not sure what path life might have taken.

In the fall of 2019, Renee Feltz and I cowrote an investigative piece about private immigrant detention (and the women leading the fight to end all detention) for *Ms.* magazine that formed the backbone for chapter 13. In addition to being an amazing cojournalist, Renee generously offered extremely helpful feedback on my immigrant detention chapter and, despite her own grueling work schedule, made time to read my entire manuscript. She always plays devil's advocate, asking questions that challenge me to dive deeper into my reporting and explanations. And she always invites me to interesting events to ensure that I leave the house and participate in the world outside of reading, writing, and caregiving.

Thank you to Melissa Morrone for carving out the time to read chapter 18 on reforms versus abolition. That chapter—as well as many others—have been shaped by our Books Through Bars packing sessions, where we sent books to incarcerated people and talked about mass incarceration late into the night. Thank you, too, for taking the time to read my entire manuscript as well as for illustrating what a continued commitment to abolition looks like in practice (such as waiting in line for six hours to give a three-minute testimony against the building of new jails!).

I am very grateful to George Francisco for listening to me talk ad nauseam about mass incarceration. Being relatively new to the issue, he asked probing questions that challenged me to clarify my arguments. Thank you, too, for sending me news articles that tied in with my work, for always being down for food, drink, and fun at the end of a long writing day, and for continual reminders to focus on the journey and not the tiny irritants along the way.

Thank you to Bryan Welton for helping me detangle some of my muddled ideas, reading chapter drafts and giving feedback that was invaluable in helping me order my thoughts. Thank you, too, for walking me (or rather texting me) through theory. You have no idea how helpful that late-night text exchange was.

Thank you to Woods Ervin for listening to me ramble about the Norwegian prison system, which helped me clarify my own thoughts, and for directing me toward policing data.

My deepest appreciation to Gayatri Patnaik and Maya Fernandez at Beacon for believing in this book and providing speedy feedback on all of my questions and drafts. Your queries and comments pushed me to dive deeper and clarify more. For that, I am extremely grateful.

Thanks, too, to Hannah Bowman, my incredible agent, who helped me navigate the complexities of book contracts and writing two books at once, and gave feedback on draft chapters. She also has gone above and beyond by reading and critiquing entire draft manuscripts, a willingness that I'm ever so appreciative of.

Many thanks and appreciation to the people currently inside prisons across the United States. Some shared their experiences with me, some took the time to read and offer feedback on chapter drafts, some pointed me toward books and articles that they thought might be useful. Thanks to Mary Fish, Kwaneta Harris, Mwalimu Shakur, Erline Bibbs, Kelly Savage, Knikita Aydelotte, Geneva Phillips, David Gilbert, Jack, Jane Dorotik, Jennifer Amelia Rose, and Marisa Simank.

While I was writing the first draft of this book, Steven had a (lifesaving) lung transplant, which required months of round-the-clock care and two subsequent hospital visits (followed by even more care!). Many friends, neighbors, and community members stepped up to help with ongoing food and respite care (including Parker, Marisa, Tauno, Melissa, Jason, Mike and Vandana, Wendy, Nanda and Jose, Miguel and Antigona, Eric and Jenna, Renee, Cale, Maya, Malav, Mark, Dan, Christine, Daniel, Marta, English Steve, Miranda, Brian and Christina, Thorn, Robert, Jen and Ari, and Julie and Rich). Without your support, I could not have written this book, and recovery would have been a much slower and more intense process. Thank you to everyone for showing us what community looks like.

Notes

INTRODUCTION

1. "Trends in U.S. Corrections," Sentencing Project, accessed March 20, 2020, https://www.sentencingproject.org/wp-content/uploads/2016/01/Trends-in-US-Corrections.pdf.

2. "Incarcerated Women and Girls," Sentencing Project, accessed March 20, 2020, https://www.sentencingproject.org/wp-content/uploads/2016/02/Incarcerated-Women-and-Girls.pdf.

3. Peter Wagner and Wendy Sawyer, "States of Incarceration: The Global Context 2018," Prison Policy Initiative, June 2018, https://www.prisonpolicy.org/global/2018.html.

4. Some prison systems have basic electronic messaging systems that incarcerated people can use to communicate with their loved ones. But the cost of sending these messages often exceeds the cost of mailing a paper letter; an electronic message of about five hundred words may cost as much as a single postage stamp. In many prisons, incarcerated people must wait in line to use a computer kiosk in the dayroom, or communal area, where they have limited time to read and respond to their messages. Meanwhile, others are waiting, sometimes impatiently and loudly, behind them.

CHAPTER 1: The system of mass incarceration is flawed and not working as designed.

1. Alexi Jones, *Correctional Control 2018: Incarceration and Supervision by State*, Prison Policy Initiative, December 2018, https://www.prisonpolicy.org/reports/correctionalcontrol2018.html.

2. Alexi Jones and Wendy Sawyer, *Arrest, Release, Repeat: How Police and Jails Are Misused to Respond to Social Problems*, Prison Policy Initiative, August 2019, https://www.prisonpolicy.org/reports/repeatarrests.html.

3. Jean Casella, "Charles Dickens on Solitary Confinement: 'Immense Torture and Agony,'" *Solitary Watch*, February 27, 2010, https://solitarywatch.org/2010/02/27/charles-dickens-on-solitary-confinement-immense-torture-and-agony.

4. Mary Ellen Curtin, *Black Prisoners and Their World: Alabama, 1865–1900*, Carter G. Woodson Institute Series in Black Studies (Charlottesville: University Press of Virginia, 2000), 6.

5. Nancy Kurshan, "Women and Imprisonment in the U.S.: History and Current Reality," http://www.freedomarchives.org/Documents/Finder/DOC3 _scans/3.kurshan.women.imprisonment.pdf, accessed April 7, 2020.

6. Richard M. Nixon, "If Mob Rule Takes Hold in the U.S.—A Warning from Richard Nixon," *U.S. News and World Report*, August 15, 1966.

7. In 1965 there were 387,390 incidents of violent crime in the United States; in 1966, the number had increased to 430,180, and in 1967 to 499,930. Department of Justice, Uniform Crime Reporting Statistics, https://www .ucrdatatool.gov/Search/Crime/Crime.cfm. According to the Brennan Center, violent crime increased 126 percent between 1960 and 1970. Lauren-Brooke Eisen and Oliver Roeder, "America's Faulty Perception of Crime Rates, March 16, 2015, https://www.brennancenter.org/blog/americas-faulty-perception -crime-rates.

8. Michelle Alexander, *The New Jim Crow: Mass Incarceration in the Age of Colorblindness* (New York: New Press, 2012), 8.

9. Alexander, *The New Jim Crow*, 50.

10. David Stein, "The Untold Story: Joe Biden Pushed Ronald Reagan to Ramp Up Incarceration—Not the Other Way Around," *Intercept*, September 17, 2019, https://theintercept.com/2019/09/17/the-untold-story-joe-biden-pushed -ronald-reagan-to-ramp-up-incarceration-not-the-other-way-around.

11. Though Clinton popularized the term, she did not create it. The term "superpredator" was created by John DeIulio Jr., a former aide to President George W. Bush. Kirsten West Savali, "For the Record: 'Superpredators' Is Absolutely a Racist Term," *Root*, September 30, 2016, https://www.theroot.com /for-the-record-superpredators-is-absolutely-a-racist-t-1790857020.

12. Carl Suddler, "How the Central Park Five Expose the Fundamental Injustice in Our Legal System," *Washington Post*, June 12, 2019, https://www .washingtonpost.com/outlook/2019/06/12/how-central-park-five-expose -fundamental-injustice-our-legal-system.

13. Eisen and Roeder, "America's Faulty Perception."

14. Carrie Johnson, "20 Years Later, Parts of Major Crime Bill Viewed as Terrible Mistake," National Public Radio, September 12, 2014, https://www.npr .org/2014/09/12/347736999/20-years-later-major-crime-bill-viewed-as -terrible-mistake.

15. David Hudson, "President Obama: 'Our Criminal Justice System Isn't as Smart as It Should Be,'" White House Archives, https://obamawhitehouse .archives.gov/blog/2015/07/15/president-obama-our-criminal-justice-system -isnt-smart-it-should-be.

16. "Clemency Statistics," US Department of Justice, https://www.justice .gov/pardon/clemency-statistics#obama, accessed April 7, 2020.

17. Arun Kundnani and Jeanne Theoharis, "Don't Expand the War on Terror in the Name of Antiracism," *Jacobin*, November 1, 2019, https://www.jacobinmag .com/2019/11/war-on-terror-domestic-terrorism-act-racism-muslims.

18. Dan Berger and Kay Whitlock, "Sanders and Warren Released Criminal Justice Plans This Week. Here's What's Good, Bad and Missing," *In These Times*,

August 23, 2019, https://inthesetimes.com/article/22026/criminal-justice
-mass-incarceration-elizabeth-warren-bernie-sanders-plan.

19. Angela Davis, *Are Prisons Obsolete?* (New York: Seven Stories Press,
2003), 16.

CHAPTER 2: We need prisons to make us safer.

1. The Sackler family had a controlling interest in Purdue Pharma, which
manufactured and launched OxyContin. At the time of this writing (September
2019), the family had been sued by at least seventeen states and had agreed to a
multimillion-dollar settlement but was not facing criminal prosecution.

2. I'll address the restorative justice system in greater detail in chapter 19.

3. Danielle Sered, *Until We Reckon: Violence, Mass Incarceration, and a Road to
Repair* (New York: New Press, 2019), 61.

4. Kamadia, letter to author, April 29, 2019.

5. Cassia Spohn and David Holleran, "The Effect of Imprisonment on Recidivism Rates of Felony Offenders: A Focus on Drug Offenders," *Criminology* 40,
no. 2 (May 2002): 329–47.

6. Mariel Alper, Matthew Durose, and Joshua Markman, *2018 Update on Prisoner Recidivism: A 9-Year Follow-Up Period (2005–2014)*, US Department of Justice,
May 2018, 1, https://www.bjs.gov/content/pub/pdf/18upr9yfup0514.pdf.

7. Alper et al., *2018 Update on Prisoner Recidivism*, 9.

8. Judith A. Greene and Vincent Schiraldi, "Better by Half: The NYC Story
of Winning Large-Scale Decarceration While Increasing Public Safety," *Federal
Sentencing Reporter* 29, no. 1 (October 2016): 23–25, https://justicestrategies.org
/Better_by_Half.

9. Marc Mauer and Nazgol Ghandnoosh, *Fewer Prisoners, Less Crime: A Tale of
3 States*, Sentencing Project, July 23, 2014, 2–6, https://www.sentencingproject
.org/publications/fewer-prisoners-less-crime-a-tale-of-three-states (New
Jersey and California statistics from this report).

10. The number of people sentenced to jail or prison dropped from 12,262
in 2017 to fewer than 10,000 in 2018. People's Lobby, "During Kim Foxx's Second Year in Office Sentences of Incarceration Decline Sharply, with No Decrease
in Public Safety," press release, July 30, 2019, https://www.thepeopleslobbyusa
.org/during-kim-foxxs-second-year-in-office-sentences-of-incarceration
-decline-sharply-with-no-decrease-in-public-safety.

11. Jonathan Ben-Menachem, "Incarceration Is Always a Policy Failure,"
Appeal, May 15, 2019, https://theappeal.org/incarceration-is-always-a-policy
-failure/#.XNwZmzOKOa4.twitter.

12. Ben-Menachem, "Incarceration Is Always a Policy Failure."

13. Legal Aid Society of New York, "Coronavirus Infection Rates as of May 8,
2020," https://legalaidnyc.org/covid-19-infection-tracking-in-nyc-jails/, accessed May 12, 2020; Legal Aid Society, "Analysis of COVID-19 Infection Rate in
NYC Jails," https://legalaidnyc.org/wp-content/uploads/2020/04/4_1_Analysis
-of-COVID-19-Infection-Rate-in-NYC-Jails.pdf, April 1, 2020.

14. Kundnani and Theoharis, "Don't Expand the War on Terror."

15. Vince Beiser, "How We Got to 2 Million: How Did the Land of the Free Become the World's Leading Jailer?" Debt to Society, MotherJones.com, special report, July 10, 2001, http://vincebeiser.com/debt-to-society/prisons_download/overview.html.

16. Robyn L. Cohen, *Prisoners in 1990*, Bureau of Justice Statistics, US Department of Justice, May 1991, https://www.bjs.gov/content/pub/pdf/p90.pdf.

17. James J. Stephan and Louis W. Jankowski, *Jail Inmates, 1990*, US Department of Justice, June 1991, https://www.bjs.gov/content/pub/pdf/ji90.pdf.

18. Darrell K. Gilliard and Allen J. Beck, *Prison and Jail Inmates, 1995*, Bureau of Justice Statistics, US Department of Justice, August 1996, https://www.bjs.gov/content/pub/pdf/PJI95.PDF.

19. 1995 and 2000 rates from Allen J. Beck and Paige M. Harrison, *Prisoners in 2000*, Bureau of Justice Statistics, US Department of Justice, August 2001, https://www.bjs.gov/content/pub/pdf/p00.pdf.

20. Heather C. West and William J. Sabol, *Prisoners in 2007* (Washington, DC: Bureau of Justice Statistics, US Department of Justice, December 2008), https://www.bjs.gov/content/pub/pdf/p07.pdf.

21. Lynn Langton et al., "Victimizations Not Reported to the Police, 2006–2010" (Washington, DC: Bureau of Justice Statistics, US Department of Justice, August 2012) 1, https://www.bjs.gov/content/pub/pdf/vnrp0610.pdf. This percentage may actually be higher since it reflects only the people who participated in the National Crime Victimization Survey.

22. "Persons Arrested," 2016 Crime in the United States, FBI, US Department of Justice, 2017, https://ucr.fbi.gov/crime-in-the-u.s/2016/crime-in-the-u.s.-2016/topic-pages/persons-arrested; "Clearances," 2016 Crime in the United States, US Department of Justice, FBI, 2017, https://ucr.fbi.gov/crime-in-the-u.s/2016/crime-in-the-u.s.-2016/topic-pages/clearances.

23. For more about victims' desire for an acknowledgment and apology for the harm that was caused, see Simmons's anthology *Love with Accountability*.

CHAPTER 3: Prisons are places of rehabilitation.

1. Mwalimu Shakur, letter to author, May 20, 2019.

2. Mwalimu Shakur, letter to author, July 30, 2019.

3. Shakur, letter to author, May 20, 2019.

4. Rand Corporation, "Education and Vocational Training Reduces Recidivism, Improves Job Outlook," August 22, 2013, http://www.rand.org/news/press/2013/08/22.html.

5. Ellen Wexler, "Prisoners to Get 'Second Chance Pell,'" *Inside Higher Ed*, June 24, 2016, https://www.insidehighered.com/news/2016/06/24/us-expands-pell-grant-program-12000-prison.

6. E. Ann Carson and Elizabeth Anderson, *Prisoners in 2015*, Bureau of Justice Statistics, US Department of Justice, December 2016, https://www.bjs.gov/content/pub/pdf/p15.pdf.

7. *Federal Prison System: FY 2021 Performance Budget Congressional Submission*, US Department of Justice, https://www.justice.gov/doj/page/file/1246231/download, page 32, accessed April 7, 2020.

8. Kamadia, letter to author, May 28, 2019.

9. Kamadia, letter to author, May 28, 2019.

10. Jack, letter to author, June 12, 2019.

11. Hazel, letter to author, June 9, 2019.

12. On January 2, 2018, CMCF had 3,428 people in custody. "Daily Inmate Population," Mississippi Department of Corrections, January 2018, https://www.mdoc.ms.gov/Admin-Finance/DailyInmatePopulation/2018-01%20Daily%20Inmate%20Population.pdf. On January 2, 2019, that number had risen to 3,882. "Daily Inmate Population," Mississippi Department of Corrections, January 2019, https://www.mdoc.ms.gov/Admin-Finance/DailyInmatePopulation/2019-01%20Daily%20Inmate%20Population.pdf.

13. Emma, letter to author, October 22, 2018; Emma, letter to author, December 16, 2018.

14. Aleks Kajstura, *States of Women's Incarceration: The Global Context 2018*, Prison Policy Initiative, June 2018, https://www.prisonpolicy.org/global/women/2018.html.

15. Kamadia, letter to author, May 28, 2019.

16. Kamadia, letter to author, July 29, 2019.

17. Mary Fish, letter to author, May 30, 2019.

18. Michelle Jones, "Incarcerated Scholars, Qualitative Inquiry, and Subjugated Knowledge: The Value of Incarcerated and Post-Incarcerated Scholars in the Age of Mass Incarceration," *Journal of Prisoners on Prisons* 25, no. 2 (2016): 103.

19. Anastazia Schmid, "'I Am Not Human in This Place': How Gynecology, Obstetrics and American Prisons Operate to Deconstruct and Control Women," *Tenacious: Art and Writings by Women in Prison* 38 (Winter 2017): 49.

CHAPTER 4: Private prison corporations drive mass incarceration.

1. Kara Gotsch and Vinay Basti, *Capitalizing on Mass Incarceration: U.S. Growth in Private Prisons*, Sentencing Project, 2018, https://www.sentencingproject.org/wp-content/uploads/2018/07/Capitalizing-on-Mass-Incarceration.pdf?eType=EmailBlastContent&eId=35b802b2-5444-4a66-9f7c-a141a75bcaf2.

2. *Criminal: How Lockup Quotas and "Low Crime Taxes" Guarantee Profits for Private Companies*, In the Public Interest, September 2013, http://www.inthepublicinterest.org/wp-content/uploads/Criminal-Lockup-Quota-Report.pdf.

3. E. Ann Carson, *Prisoners in 2018*, Table 18, Bureau of Justice Statistics, US Department of Justice, April 2020, https://www.bjs.gov/content/pub/pdf/p18.pdf.

4. "Prisoners in 1983," *Bureau of Justice Statistics Bulletin*, April 1984, https://www.bjs.gov/content/pub/pdf/p83.pdf.

5. David Dayen, "The Private Prison Divestment Movement Just Had an Incredible Week," *In These Times*, March 14, 2019, http://inthesetimes.com /article/21793/private-prison-divestment-jpmorgan-ocasio-cortez-wells-fargo.

6. "As Wall Street Banks Sever Ties, Private Prison Companies Stand to Lose Over $1.9B in Future Financing," Center for Popular Democracy, July 17, 2019, https://populardemocracy.org/news/publications/wall-street-banks-sever -ties-private-prison-companies-stand-lose-over-19b-future.

7. Andrea Castillo, "California Bans For-Profit Prisons and Immigration Detention Facilities," *Los Angeles Times*, October 11, 2019, https://www.latimes .com/california/story/2019-10-11/california-bans-for-profit-prisons-and -immigrant-detention-facilities.

8. Madison Pauly, "The Private Prison Industry Just Suffered a Major Blow. And It Could Just Be the Beginning," *Mother Jones*, March 7, 2019, https://www .motherjones.com/crime-justice/2019/03/jp-morgan-chase-divestment -private-prisons-lauren-brooke-eisen.

9. *Criminal: How Lock-Up Quotas and "Low-Crime Taxes" Guarantee Profits for Private Prison Corporations.*

10. "Core Civic Inc," OpenSecrets.org, https://www.opensecrets.org/orgs /summary.php?id=D000021940&cycle=2018, accessed April 8, 2020; "GEO Group," OpenSecrets.org, https://www.opensecrets.org/orgs/summary.php ?cycle=2018&id=D000022003, accessed April 8, 2020.

11. Brigette Sarabi and Edwin Bender, *The Prison Payoff: The Role of Politics and Private Prisons in the Incarceration Boom*, Western States Center and Western Prison Project, Prison Policy Initiative, 2000, https://www.prisonpolicy.org /scans/Prison_Payoff_Report_WPP_2000.pdf.

12. Bryan Welton, "Reimagining and Repurposing Divestment," *Abolitionist*, no. 26 (Summer 2016), https://abolitionistpaper.files.wordpress.com/2017/04 /the-abolitionist-issue-26.pdf.

13. Craig Gilmore, "On the Business of Incarceration," *Commune*, July 12, 2019, https://communemag.com/on-the-business-of-incarceration.

14. Victoria Law, "What Do Private Prisons Have to Do with the Upcoming Election?," *Truthout*, October 28, 2014, https://truthout.org/articles/what-do -private-prisons-have-to-do-with-the-upcoming-election.

15. *The 2017–18 Budget: California Department of Corrections and Rehabilitation*, Legal Analyst's Office, March 1, 2017, https://lao.ca.gov/Publications/Report/3595.

16. Austin McCoy, "Prison Guard Unions and Mass Incarceration: Prospects for an Improbable Alliance," *New Labor Forum* 26, no. 1 (2017): 78, https:// journals.sagepub.com/doi/full/10.1177/1095796016681558.

17. Whet Moser, "Why Labor Is Fighting Tamms Prison Closure," *Chicago Magazine*, February 27, 2013, https://www.chicagomag.com/Chicago-Magazine /The-312/February-2013/Why-Labor-Is-Fighting-the-Tamms-Prison-Closure. Ultimately, the state supreme court ruled against the union, and Tamms was closed in 2013.

18. J. T. Stapleton, "Names in the News: Correction Officers' Benevolent Association," FollowTheMoney.org, March 23, 2013, https://www.followthemoney

.org/research/institute-reports/names-in-the-news-police-officers-benevolent -association.

19. "New York Correctional Officers and Police Benevolent Association," FollowingtheMoney.org, https://www.followthemoney.org/entity-details?eid =18929866, accessed April 9, 2020.

20. Ruth Wilson Gilmore in conversation with Rachel Kushner, Lannan Podcasts, April 17, 2019, https://podcast.lannan.org/2019/04/21/ruth-wilson -gilmore-with-rachel-kushner-conversation-17-april-2019-video.

21. Sally Q. Yates, "Phasing Out Our Use of Private Prisons," US Department of Justice, August 18, 2016, https://www.justice.gov/archives/opa/blog/phasing -out-our-use-private-prisons.

22. Sally Q. Yates to Acting Director of Federal Bureau of Prisons, "Memo: Reducing Our Use of Private Prisons," August 18, 2016, https://www.justice.gov /archives/opa/file/886311/download.

23. Victoria Law, "Private Prisons Are Far from Ended: 62 Percent of Im- migrant Detainees Are in Privatized Jails," *Truthout*, August 19, 2016, https:// truthout.org/articles/private-prisons-are-far-from-ended-62-percent-of -immigrant-detainees-are-in-privatized-jails.

24. Victoria Law, "Will Obama's Commutation Allow Grandma Hardy and Thousands of Drug War Prisoners to Finally Go Home?" *Truthout*, August 20, 2014, https://truthout.org/news/item/25497-will-obamas-commutation -allow-grandma-hardy-and-thousands-of-drug-war-prisoners-to-finally -go-home.

25. Law, "What Do Private Prisons Have to Do with the Upcoming Election?"

26. Eric Lichtblau, "Justice Department Keeps For-Profit Prisons, Scrap- ping an Obama Plan," *New York Times*, February 23, 2017, https://www.nytimes .com/2017/02/23/us/politics/justice-department-private-prisons.html.

27. Carson, *Prisoners in 2018*, Table 18.

28. "CoreCivic Reports Fourth Quarter and Full Year 2018 Financial Re- sults," CoreCivic, February 19, 2019, http://ir.corecivic.com/news-releases /news-release-details/corecivic-reports-fourth-quarter-and-full-year-2018 -financial.

29. "The GEO Group Reports Fourth Quarter and Full-Year 2018 Results," press release, GEO Group, February 14, 2019, https://platform.mi.spglobal.com /IRW/file/4144107/Index?KeyFile=396741829.

30. *The 2018–19 Budget: California Spending Plan*, Legislative Analyst's Office, https://lao.ca.gov/Publications/Report/3870/11.

31. Peter Wagner, "Are Private Prisons Driving Mass Incarceration?," Prison Policy Initiative, October 7, 2015, https://www.prisonpolicy.org/blog /2015/10/07/private_prisons_parasite.

CHAPTER 5: Private corporations and profit from prison labor drive mass incarceration.

1. Wendy Sawyer and Peter Wagner, *Mass Incarceration: The Whole Pie 2019*, Prison Policy Initiative, March 19, 2019, https://www.prisonpolicy.org/reports /pie2019.html.

2. Ruth Wilson Gilmore in conversation with Rachel Kushner, Lannan Podcasts, April 17, 2019, https://podcast.lannan.org/2019/04/21/ruth-wilson-gilmore-with-rachel-kushner-conversation-17-april-2019-video.

3. Nicole Hahn Rafter, *Partial Justice: Women, Prisons, and Social Control*, 2nd ed. (New Brunswick: Transaction Publishers, 1990), 9.

4. Curtin, *Black Prisoners and Their World*, 6. In 1865, $50 would be the equivalent of $788 in 2020. Thirty cents in 1865 would be the equivalent of $4.73 in 2020.

5. Clifford Young, *Women's Prisons: Past and Present and Other New York State Prison History* (Elmira Reformatory, NY: Summary Press, 1932), 4.

6. Nicole Hahn Rafter, "Prisons for Women," *Crime and Justice* 5 (1983): 139, https://www.jstor.org/stable/1147471?mag=history-of-womens-prisons&seq=7#metadata_info_tab_contents.

7. Rafter, *Partial Justice*, 18–19.

8. Rafter, *Partial Justice*, 18–19. Cites Mount Pleasant State Prison, *AR of the Inspectors 1846* (New York Sen. Doc. No. 16, 1846): Appendix D, 88.

9. John McCoy and Ethan Hoffman, *Concrete Mama: Prison Profiles from Walla Walla* (Columbia: University of Missouri Press, 1981), 134–35.

10. Amnesty International, *Edge of Endurance* (London: Peter Benenson House, 2012), 15.

11. Christopher Robbins, "New York State's New Hand Sanitizer Is Made By Prisoners Paid an Average of 65 Cents an Hour," *Gothamist*, March 9, 2020, https://gothamist.com/news/new-york-states-new-hand-sanitizer-made-prisoners-paid-average-65-cents-hour.

12. Though Corcraft cannot sell to private sectors, the company's 2013 revenue was nearly $48 million. Revenue from the sales go into the state's general fund, not into any corporation's pocket. "No Wage Increase for Dime-an-Hour New York Inmates," CNY Central, January 25, 2013, http://cnycentral.com/news/local/no-wage-increase-for-dime-an-hour-new-york-inmates.

13. Sawyer and Wagner, *Mass Incarceration*.

14. "UNICOR: Program Details," Federal Bureau of Prisons, https://www.bop.gov/inmates/custody_and_care/unicor_about.jsp, accessed April 9, 2020.

15. James Kilgore, "Confronting Prison Slave Labor Camps and Other Myths," *Social Justice Journal*, August 28, 2013, http://www.socialjusticejournal.org/confronting-prison-slave-labor-camps-and-other-myths.

16. Victoria Law, "Investigation: Corporations Are Profiting from Immigrant Detainees' Labor. Some Say It's Slavery," *In These Times*, May 29, 2018, http://inthesetimes.com/features/ice_immigrant_detention_centers_forced_prison_labor_investigation.html.

17. In 2018 Colorado voters approved Amendment A, a constitutional amendment removing the Thirteenth Amendment's exception for those convicted of a crime. It was the first state to do so.

18. Margie Wood, "DOC Pilot Program Working Well," *Pueblo Chieftain*, July 11, 2007, http://beta.chieftain.com/opinion/editorials/good-work/article_9ba41d40-99f6-11df-b814-001cc4c002e0.html.

19. Christopher Zoukis, "The Taste of Exploitation: Whole Foods Carrying Products Made by Prisoners," *Prison Legal News*, July 6, 2016, https://www.prisonlegalnews.org/news/2016/jul/6/taste-exploitation-whole-foods-stops-carrying-products-made-prisoners.

20. Jenny, letter to author, February 27, 2019.

21. Martha, letter to author, February 6, 2019.

22. In December 2019, after an article in *The Intercept* revealed that women incarcerated at Eddie Warrior Correctional Center were making campaign calls on behalf of former New York City mayor and presidential candidate Michael Bloomberg, ProCom discontinued its political surveys and campaign calls. The company did not cease all operations, although it began enforcing its requirement that incarcerated workers turn in their phone scripts after each shift. See John Washington, "Mike Bloomberg Exploited Prison Labor to Make 2020 Presidential Campaign Phone Calls," *Intercept*, December 24, 2019, https://theintercept.com/2019/12/24/mike-bloomberg-2020-prison-labor.

23. Martha, letter to author, January 29, 2019.

24. Martha, letter to author, April 3, 2019.

25. In January 2019 Democratic senator George Young introduced a bill to raise Oklahoma's minimum wage to $10.50 per hour.

26. Kilgore, "Confronting Prison Slave Labor Camps."

27. Sawyer and Wagner, *Mass Incarceration*.

28. Kilgore, "Confronting Prison Slave Labor Camps."

29. Martha, letter to author, October 22, 2019.

30. Martha, letter to author, September 4, 2019.

31. Martha, letter to author, March 26, 2019.

32. Martha, letter to author, April 12, 2019.

33. I am borrowing the term "prison slave labor camps" from Kilgore's "Confronting Prison Slave Labor Camps."

34. "Who Is CCI," Colorado Correctional Industries, https://www.coloradoci.com/bin-htm/aboutUs.html?intro, accessed April 9, 2020.

35. As of September 2019, Colorado had 19,748 state prisoners. *Departmental Reports and Statistics*, Colorado Department of Corrections, April 9, 2020, https://www.colorado.gov/pacific/cdoc/departmental-reports-and-statistics.

36. As of October 14, 2019, the Eddie Warrior Correctional Center held 985 women. Oklahoma Department of Corrections, Weekly Count, week ending October 14, 2019, accessed October 15, 2019, http://doc.ok.gov/Websites/doc/images/Documents/Population/Count%20Sheet/2019/DOC%20OMS%20Count%2010-14-19.pdf.

37. Martha, letter to author, February 6, 2019.

38. Martha, letter to author, February 14, 2019.

39. Martha, letter to the author, March 26, 2019.

CHAPTER 6: Race has nothing to do with mass incarceration.

1. Josie Duffy Rice and Clint Smith, "Justice in America Episode 20: Mariame Kaba and Prison Abolition," *Appeal*, March 20, 2019, https://theappeal.org

/justice-in-america-episode-20-mariame-kaba-and-prison-abolition/#
.XJJG6MWRzFI.twitter.

2. Carson, *Prisoners in 2018*, Table 9, page 15, https://www.bjs.gov/content
/pub/pdf/p18.pdf.

3. "Quick Facts: United States," US Census Bureau, https://www.census.gov
/quickfacts/fact/table/US/RHI225217#RHI225217, accessed April 9, 2020.

4. Carson, *Prisoners in 2018*, Table 9, page 15.

5. Carson, *Prisoners in 2018*, Table 10, page 16.

6. "Justice Department Announces Findings of Investigation into Baltimore
Police Department," US Department of Justice, August 10, 2016, https://www
.justice.gov/opa/pr/justice-department-announces-findings-investigation
-baltimore-police-department; "Latest Court Filing Shows Race Still Plays a
Role in Stops and Frisks by Police in Philadelphia," ACLU of Pennsylvania, November 27, 2018, https://www.aclupa.org/news/2018/11/27/latest-court-filing
-shows-race-still-plays-role-stops-and-fr; "Stop-and-Frisk Data," ACLU of New
York, https://www.nyclu.org/en/stop-and-frisk-data, accessed March 6, 2019.

7. Jaime M. Grant el al., *Injustice at Every Turn: A Report of The National
Transgender Discrimination Survey*, National Center for Transgender Equality and
National Gay and Lesbian Task Force, 2011, https://www.transequality.org/sites
/default/files/docs/resources/NTDS_Report.pdf, 163.

8. Duffy Rice and Smith, "Justice in America."

9. J. Henry Brown, *Brown's Political History of Oregon: Provisional Government*
(Portland, OR: Wiley B. Allen, 1892), https://archive.org/stream/browns
politicaloounkngoog#page/n9/mode/2up.

10. "The History of Mass Incarceration with Kelly Lytle Hernandez," WORT
Local News, February 22, 2019, https://www.wortfm.org/the-history-of-mass
-incarceration-with-kelly-lytle-hernandez/#.XHCKUnX96tQ.twitter.

11. "Quick Facts: United States," US Census Bureau, https://www.census.
gov/quickfacts/fact/table/US/RHI725217#RHI725217, accessed April 9, 2020.

12. E. Ann Carson, *Prisoners in 2016*, US Department of Justice, January 2018,
page 7, https://www.bjs.gov/content/pub/pdf/p16.pdf. Carson, *Prisoners in 2018*,
lumps Native Americans in with all races that are not Black, white, or Hispanic.

13. Alexander, *The New Jim Crow*, 135.

14. "Stop-and-Frisk Data," ACLU of New York.

15. Joseph Goldstein, "Judge Rejects New York's Stop-and-Frisk Policy,"
New York Times, August 12, 2013, https://www.nytimes.com/2013/08/13/ny
region/stop-and-frisk-practice-violated-rights-judge-rules.html.

16. On May 6, 2015, after decades of organizing by Chicago activists, the city
council passed SR2015-256, which recognized that Burge and his police force
had subjected hundreds to police-sanctioned torture. SR2015-256 awarded each
survivor up to one hundred thousand dollars, free tuition at the city's community
colleges, and free psychological counseling. It also promised to erect a memorial
to the city's torture survivors and to include curriculum on the Burge case and its
legacy in all city public schools. Peter C. Baker, "In Chicago, Reparations Aren't

Just an Idea. They're the Law," *Guardian*, March 8, 2019, https://www.theguardian
.com/news/2019/mar/08/chicago-reparations-won-police-torture-school
-curriculum.

17. Spencer Ackerman, "Homan Square Revealed: How Chicago Police 'Disappeared' 7,000 People," *Guardian*, October 19, 2015, https://www.theguardian.com
/us-news/2015/oct/19/homan-square-chicago-police-disappeared-thousands.

18. Michelle Alexander, "Reckoning with Violence," *New York Times*, March
3, 2019, https://www.nytimes.com/2019/03/03/opinion/violence-criminal
-justice.html.

19. Alexander, "Reckoning with Violence."

20. Aviva Stahl, "NYPD Undercover 'Converted' to Islam to Spy on Brooklyn
College Students," *Gothamist*, October 29, 2015, https://gothamist.com/news
/nypd-undercover-converted-to-islam-to-spy-on-brooklyn-college-students;
Michael Silber and Arvin Bhatt, *Radicalization in the West: The Homegrown Threat*
(New York Police Department, 2007), http://www.nyc.gov/html/nypd/downloads
/pdf/public_information/NYPD_Report-Radicalization_in_the_West.pdf.

21. George Brown, "Notes on a Terrorism Trial: Preventive Prosecution,
'Material Support' and the Role of the Judge in *United States v. Mehanna*," *Harvard
National Security Journal* 4, no. 1 (2012), http://harvardnsj.org/wp-content
/uploads/2013/01/Vol-4-Brown-FINAL.pdf.

22. Spencer Ackerman, "Shahawar Matin Siraj: 'Impressionable' Young Man
Caught in an NYPD Sting," *Guardian*, July 21, 2014, https://www.theguardian
.com/world/2014/jul/21/shahawar-matin-siraj-impressionable-nypd-sting.
See also Human Rights Watch, *Illusion of Justice: Human Rights Abuses in US Terrorism Prosecutions*, Columbia Law School, Human Rights Institute, July 2014, 27.

23. Victoria Law, "No Separate Justice Campaign Denounces Post 9/11
Abuses," *Waging Nonviolence*, September 11, 2014, https://wagingnonviolence
.org/2014/09/separate-justice.

24. Alexander, *The New Jim Crow*, 115.

25. *Cracks in the System: Twenty Years of the Unjust Federal Crack Cocaine Law*
(American Civil Liberties Union, October 2006), https://www.aclu.org/other
/cracks-system-20-years-unjust-federal-crack-cocaine-law.

26. Alexander, *The New Jim Crow*, 113–14.

27. Alexander, *The New Jim Crow*, 115.

28. Joshua Vaughn, "In a Pennsylvania County, Black Children are Disproportionately Charged in Adult Court," *Appeal*, November 27, 2018, https://the
appeal.org/in-pennsylvania-county-black-kids-are-disproportionately
-charged-in-adult-court.

29. Breonna Taylor, George Floyd, and Tony McDade were all Black people
killed by the police in 2020. Breonna Taylor was fatally shot by Louisville police
in her own home on March 13, 2020. On May 25, 2020, Minneapolis police
officer Derek Chauvin knelt on George Floyd's neck for eight minutes and 46
seconds, killing him. On May 27, 2020, Tony McDade, a trans man, was killed by
Tallahassee police. Following weeks of protests, the Minneapolis City Council voted

to defund the police, the Seattle City Council voted to defund the police by 50 percent, and the City Council of Norman, Oklahoma, voted to reallocate $865,000 (or 3.6 percent) of the police budget to community development programs.

CHAPTER 7: "Don't do the crime if you can't do the time": People need to take personal responsibility for their actions.

1. Knikita Aydelotte, letter to author, May 29, 2019.

2. Jennifer Amelia Rose, letter to author, June 21, 2019.

3. Ashley Nellis, *Still Life: America's Increasing Use of Life and Long-Term Sentences* (Sentencing Project, May 2017), https://www.sentencingproject.org /publications/still-life-americas-increasing-use-life-long-term-sentences /#III.%20Life%20by%20the%20Numbers.

4. Nellis, *Still Life.*

5. Victoria Law, "Suicide of 70-Year-Old John Mackenzie After Tenth Parole Denial Illustrates Broken System," *Village Voice*, August 9, 2016, https://www .villagevoice.com/2016/08/09/suicide-of-70-year-old-john-mackenzie-after -tenth-parole-denial-illustrates-broken-system.

6. "A Challenge to New York's Broken Parole Board," editorial, *New York Times*, June 13, 2016, http://www.nytimes.com/2016/06/13/opinion/a-challenge -to-new-yorks-broken-parole-board.html.

7. Law, "Suicide of 70-Year-Old John Mackenzie Mackenzie After Tenth Parole Denial Illustrates Broken System."

8. "Building Bridges," *Prison Action Newsletter*, July–August 2016, http:// prisonaction.blogspot.com/2016/08/julyaugust-2016_90.html.

9. New York State Department of Corrections and Community Supervision, *2011 Inmate Releases: Three Year Post-Release Follow-Up*, http://www.doccs.ny.gov /Research/Reports/2016/2011_releases_3yr_out.pdf, accessed September 25, 2019.

10. Sered, *Until We Reckon*, 39–40.

11. Sissy, letter to author, postmarked June 9, 2019.

12. Tim Lockette, "Alabama Often Denies Prisoners Parole, But Doesn't Tell Them Why," *Anniston Star*, April 11, 2015, http://www.annistonstar.com/news /alabama-often-denies-prisoners-parole-but-doesn-t-tell-them/article_79e3fd36 -e0a2-11e4-b478-2ba6ccad8092.html.

13. Aydelotte, letter to author, May 29, 2019.

CHAPTER 8: Jails and prisons provide people with needed mental health care.

1. Matt Ford, "America's Largest Mental Health Hospital Is a Jail," *Atlantic*, June 8, 2015, https://www.theatlantic.com/politics/archive/2015/06/americas -largest-mental-hospital-is-a-jail/395012.

2. "The Largest Jails in the United States," World Atlas, updated September 28, 2017, https://www.worldatlas.com/articles/the-largest-jails-in-the-united -states.html.

3. "Jailing People with Mental Illness," National Alliance on Mental Illness, https://www.nami.org/Learn-More/Public-Policy/Jailing-People-with-Mental -Illness, accessed April 9, 2020.

4. Ford, "America's Largest Mental Health Hospital Is a Jail."

5. Ford, "America's Largest Mental Health Hospital Is a Jail."

6. Terry Kupers, "A New Mental Health Jail vs. Community Mental Health Treatment," *Los Angeles Daily News*, February 10, 2019, https://www.dailynews.com/2019/02/10/a-new-mental-health-jail-vs-community-mental-health-treatment.

7. Kupers, "A New Mental Health Jail vs. Community Mental Health Treatment."

8. Azu AbuDagga, Sidney Wolfe, Michael Carome, Amanda Phatdouang, and E. Fuller Torrey, *Individuals with Serious Mental Illnesses in County Jails: A Survey of Jail Staff's Perspectives* (Public Citizen's Health Research Group and the Treatment Advocacy Center, 2016), 11, https://www.treatmentadvocacycenter.org/storage/documents/jail-survey-report-2016.pdf.

9. Patrisse Khan-Cullors, *When They Call You a Terrorist: A Black Lives Matter Memoir* (New York: St. Martin's Press, 2018), 116.

10. Khan-Cullors, *When They Call You a Terrorist*, 117–18.

11. After three months in the jail, a court deemed Ms. DM incompetent and unrestorable to stand trial. She was transferred to the Desert Vista psychiatric facility. Graves v. Arpaio, No. CV-77-479-PHX-NVW, May 8, 2014, 78, 106, https://www.aclu.org/sites/default/files/field_document/2269_pls_post-trial_proposed_findings_of_fact_and_col_5.8.14.pdf.

12. Kupers, "A New Mental Health Jail vs. Community Mental Health Treatment."

13. "Postpartum Depression: Symptoms and Causes," Mayo Clinic, September 1, 2018, https://www.mayoclinic.org/diseases-conditions/postpartum-depression/symptoms-causes/syc-20376617.

14. Margaret Majos, *I Did Not Die* (Maitland, FL: Xulon Press, 2009), 40.

15. In 2018, there were seventeen attempted suicides and no actual suicides at CIW. California Department of Corrections and Rehabilitation (CDCR), *Female Offenders: COMPSTAT DAI Statistical Report—13 Month*, https://www.cdcr.ca.gov/research/wp-content/uploads/sites/174/2019/10/2019_05_DAI-Female-Offenders.pdf, accessed October 29, 2019.

16. CDCR, *Female Offenders*.

17. Victoria Law, "'Out of the Blue': Loved Ones Search for Answers in Shaylene Graves' Prison Death," *Truthout*, July 31, 2016, https://truthout.org/articles/out-of-the-blue-loved-ones-search-for-answers-in-shaylene-graves-prison-death.

18. Victoria Law, "Erika Rocha's Suicide Brings Attention to the Dire Need for Mental Health Care in Prison," *Rewire News*, May 20, 2016, https://rewire.news/article/2016/05/20/erika-rochas-suicide-brings-attention-dire-need-mental-health-care-prison.

19. Venters, *Life and Death on Rikers Island*, 95–96.

20. Victoria Law, "'There's Still a Serious Crisis in Black America': Patrisse Khan-Cullors on Breaking the Silence," *Rewire News*, February 5, 2018, https://rewire.news/article/2018/02/05/theres-still-serious-crisis-black-america-patrisse-khan-cullors-breaking-silence.

CHAPTER 9: People in prison "jump the line" for life-saving medical care.

1. "Prisoner Gets $1M Heart Transplant," CBS News, January 31, 2002, https://www.cbsnews.com/news/prisoner-gets-1m-heart-transplant; Katie Moisse, "NC Man Allegedly Robs Bank of $1 to Get Health Care in Jail," ABC News, June 20, 2011, https://abcnews.go.com/Health/Wellness/nc-man-allegedly-robs-bank-health-care-jail/story?id=13887040; Bryan Robinson, "Death-Row Inmate Seeks Organ Transplant," ABC News, https://abcnews.go.com/US/story?id=90611&page=1.

2. Homer Venters, quoted in Jennifer Gonnerman's "Do Jails Kill People?," *New Yorker*, February 20, 2019, https://www.newyorker.com/books/under-review/do-jails-kill-people.

3. Venters, quoted in Gonnerman's "Do Jails Kill People?"

4. Legal Aid Society of New York, *Analysis of COVID-19 Infection Rate in NYC Jails, Including Rikers Island*, March 25, 2020, https://legalaidnyc.org/wp-content/uploads/2020/03/3_25_Analysis-of-COVID-19-Infection-Rate-in-NYC-Jails.pdf; Legal Aid Society of New York, *Analysis of COVID-19 Infection Rate in NYC Jails*, May 1, 2020, https://legalaidnyc.org/wp-content/uploads/2020/05/5_1_Analysis-of-COVID-19-Infection-Rate-in-NYC-Jails.pdf.

5. Reuven Blau and Rosa Goldensohn, "Rikers Inmates Pepper Sprayed for Demanding Medical Care, Sources Say," *The City*, March 23, 2020, https://thecity.nyc/2020/03/rikers-inmates-pepper-sprayed-for-medical-care-plea-sources.html.

6. Eddie Small, "Rikers Jail Medical Provider Let Inmate Die from Diabetic Coma, Suit Says," *DNA Info*, August 21, 2014, https://www.dnainfo.com/new-york/20140821/hunts-point/rikers-jail-medical-provider-let-inmate-die-from-diabetic-coma-suit-says.

7. Michael Schwirtz and Michael Winerip, "An Unanswered Call for Help," *New York Times*, September 1, 2015, https://www.nytimes.com/2015/09/02/nyregion/an-unanswered-call-for-help-at-rikers-island.html.

8. Zachariah Bryan, "County Settles for $3.1M in Woman's Jail-Related Death," *South Whidbey Record*, September 17, 2019, http://www.southwhidbeyrecord.com/news/county-settles-for-3-1m-in-womans-jail-related-death.

9. Mark Wilson and Matthew Clarke, "Jails in Oregon and Washington State Have High Prisoner Death Rates," *Prison Legal News*, September 5, 2019, https://www.prisonlegalnews.org/news/2019/sep/5/jails-oregon-and-washington-state-have-high-prisoner-death-rates.

10. Kamadia, letter to author, April 1, 2019.

11. In February 2019, California legislation eliminated co-pays in the state's prison system. County jails, however, are still allowed to charge medical co-pays to people in custody. *State and Federal Prison Co-Pay Policies and Sourcing Information*, Prison Policy Initiative, https://www.prisonpolicy.org/reports/copay_policies.html, accessed April 9, 2020.

12. Wendy Sawyer, *The Steep Cost of Medical Co-Pays in Prison Puts Health at Risk*, Prison Policy Initiative, April 19, 2017, https://www.prisonpolicy.org/blog/2017/04/19/copays.

13. *State and Federal Prison Wage Policies and Sourcing Information*, Prison Policy Initiative, https://www.prisonpolicy.org/reports/wage_policies.html, accessed April 9, 2020.

14. Maurice Chammah, "Some Inmates Forego Health Care to Avoid Fees," *Texas Tribune*, October 16, 2012, https://www.texastribune.org/2012/10/16/tdcj -inmates-paying-100-fee-health-care.

15. Max Rivlin-Nadler, "Texas May Double Healthcare Fees for Its Massive Prison Population," *Vice*, February 23, 2017, https://www.vice.com/en_us/article /vvqw9d/texas-may-double-healthcare-fees-for-its-massive-prison-population.

16. Gongwer News Service, "Corizon Fined $1.6 Million for Violations of Michigan's Corrections Department Health Contract," *Crain's Detroit Business*, February 21, 2019, https://www.crainsdetroit.com/health-care/corizon-fined -16-million-violations-michigan-corrections-department-health-contract.

17. "Corizon Health Registered Nurse Hourly Pay," Glassdoor, updated February 3, 2020, https://www.glassdoor.com/Hourly-Pay/Corizon-Health -Registered-Nurse-Hourly-Pay-E419429_D_KO15,31.htm.

18. "California Department of Corrections and Rehabilitation Registered Nurse Hourly Pay," Glassdoor, updated May 23, 2019, https://www.glassdoor.com /Salary/California-Department-of-Corrections-and-Rehabilitation-Registered -Nurse-Salaries-E41905_D_KO56,72.htm.

19. Gongwer, "Corizon Fined $1.6 Million."

20. Kristen Jordan Shamus, "Michigan Spending One-Fifth of Its General Fund Budget on Prisoners," *Detroit Free Press*, December 19, 2018, https://www .freep.com/story/news/local/michigan/2018/12/19/prison-michigan-corrections -jail/2230794002.

21. "About Corizon Health," Corizon Health, http://www.corizonhealth.com /About-Corizon/Locations, accessed February 28, 2019.

22. "History," Wexford Health Sources, http://www.wexfordhealth.com/About -Us/History, accessed February 29, 2019.

23. HIG Capital, "Portfolio: Wellpath," https://higcapital.com/portfolio /company/403, accessed May 2, 2020.

24. Venters, *Life and Death on Rikers Island*, 72.

25. Venters, *Life and Death on Rikers Island*, 79.

26. Venters, *Life and Death on Rikers Island*, 17.

27. American Association for the Study of Liver Diseases and Infectious Diseases Society of America, *HCV Treatment and Testing in Correctional Settings*, https:// www.hcvguidelines.org/unique-populations/correctional, accessed May 29, 2020.

28. Fox Butterfield, "U.S. Prisons Turning into Incubators for Infectious Diseases/HIV, Hepatitis C, Tuberculosis Rampant," *SF Gate*, February 2, 2003, http://www.sfgate.com/news/article/U-S-prisons-turning-into-incubators -for-2675781.php.

29. Associated Press, "2013: Gilead's Breakthrough Hepatitis C Drug Approved by the FDA," *Mercury News*, December 6, 2013, https://www.mercurynews .com/2013/12/06/2013-gileads-breakthrough-hepatitis-c-drug-approved-by-fda.

30. Michelle Andrews, "FDA's Approval of a Cheaper Drug for Hepatitis C Will Likely Expand Treatment," National Public Radio, October 4, 2017, https://www.npr.org/sections/health-shots/2017/10/04/555156577/fdas-approval-of-a-cheaper-drug-for-hepatitis-c-will-likely-expand-treatment.

31. "Prison Spending in 2015," in *The Price of Prisons* (New York: Vera Institute of Justice, May 2017), https://www.vera.org/publications/price-of-prisons-2015-state-spending-trends/price-of-prisons-2015-state-spending-trends/price-of-prisons-2015-state-spending-trends-prison-spending, accessed April 9, 2020.

32. Jeff Bernstein, *Incarceration Trends in Massachusetts: Long-Term Increases, Recent Progress* (Massachusetts Budget and Policy Center, January 26, 2016), http://www.massbudget.org/reports/pdf/Incarceration%20Trends%20in%20Massachusetts%20Long-term%20Increases,%20Recent%20Progress%201-26-2016.pdf, 5.

33. Fowler v. Turco, C.A. No. 1:15CV12298, May 16, 2016, https://www.docketbird.com/court-documents/Fowler-et-al-v-Turco-et-al/AMENDED-COMPLAINT-against-Massachusetts-Partnership-for-Correctional-Healthcare-LLC-Thomas-Turco-filed-by-Jeffrey-Fowler-Paul-R-Whooten-Michael-Turner-Michael-Fitzpatrick/mad-1:2015-cv-12298-00049.

34. By then, Paszko had died of hepatitis C complications. Jeffrey Fowler was treated before the suit reached settlement.

35. Marshall Project, "A State-by-State Look at Coronavirus in Prisons," https://www.themarshallproject.org/2020/05/01/a-state-by-state-look-at-coronavirus-in-prisons, accessed September 15, 2020.

36. Victoria Law, "Being in Prison May No Longer Be a Barrier to Receiving Treatment for Hepatitis C—At Least If You're in Prison," *The Body*, July 12, 2018, https://www.thebody.com/content/81150/being-in-prison-may-no-longer-be-a-barrier-to-rece.html.

CHAPTER 10: Prison is an effective way to get people into drug treatment.

1. Maggie Luna, interview with author, April 11, 2019.

2. Kamadia, letter to author, April 29, 2019.

3. Susan Burton, *Becoming Ms. Burton* (New York: New Press, 2018).

4. Victoria Law, "From Revolving Door to Re-Entry: An Interview with Susan Burton," *Truthout*, May 14, 2017, https://truthout.org/articles/from-revolving-door-to-reentry-an-interview-with-susan-burton.

5. Kamadia, letter to author, May 28, 2019.

6. Elizabeth Weill-Greenberg, "Overdose in an Arizona Prison? Get Ready to Pay Up," *Appeal*, May 3, 2019, https://theappeal.org/prisoners-in-arizona-now-charged-for-their-own-drug-related-hospital-visits/#.XNZgV20VKgL.twitter.

7. Weill-Greenberg, "Overdose in an Arizona Prison?"

8. Weill-Greenberg, "Overdose in an Arizona Prison?"

9. Arizona Department of Corrections, *Department Order Manual*, Chapter 800: "Inmate Management," amended March 15, 2019, https://corrections.az .gov/sites/default/files/policies/800/0803_032519.pdf, p. 16.

10. Law, "From Revolving Door to Re-Entry."

CHAPTER 11: Mass incarceration only affects Black cisgender men.

1. *Incarcerated Women and Girls*, Sentencing Project, June 6, 2019, https:// www.sentencingproject.org/publications/incarcerated-women-and-girls.

2. Carson, *Prisoners in 2018*, p. 3.

3. Zhen Zeng, *Jail Inmates in 2018* (Washington, DC: US Department of Justice), March 2020, Table 3, https://www.bjs.gov/content/pub/pdf/ji18.pdf; Carson, *Prisoners in 2018*, Table 9.

4. Ilan H. Meyer et al., "Incarceration Rates and Traits of Sexual Minorities in the United States: National Inmate Survey, 2011–2012," *American Journal of Public Health* 107, no. 2 (February 2017), https://www.ncbi.nlm.nih.gov/pmc /articles/PMC5227944.

5. In 2015, Shiloh Quine, a trans women serving life without parole in California, successfully sued for gender-affirming surgery. She was subsequently transferred from a men's to a women's prison. In December 2018, the Illinois Department of Corrections transferred Strawberry Hampton—who had served four years of her ten-year sentence in the state's male prisons where she had been physically and sexually assaulted—to a women's prison.

6. Allen J. Beck, "Supplemental Tables: Prevalence of Sexual Victimization Among Transgender Adult Inmates," in *Sexual Victimization in Prisons and Jails Reported by Inmates, 2011–12* (US Department of Justice, Bureau of Justice Statistics, December 2014), https://www.hivlawandpolicy.org/sites/default/files /Sexual%20Victimization%20in%20Prisons%20and%20Jails%20Supplemental %20Tables.pdf.

7. In November, 2017 the New York City Department of Correction, which operates the city's jail system, began tracking the housing placements of people who identified as trans, gender non-conforming, and intersex. As of April 2019, the city's jails had identified fifty trans women in its custody. Of those fifty, only half were in the Trans Housing Unit, a designated unit for trans women. The remaining half were housed in men's jails.

8. Melissa Gira Grant, "'The Police Act Like We Are Nothing,'" *Appeal*, February 25, 2019, https://theappeal.org/the-police-act-like-we-are-nothing/.

9. Jaime M. Grant el al., *Injustice at Every Turn: A Report of the National Transgender Discrimination Survey* (2011), https://www.transequality.org/sites/default /files/docs/resources/NTDS_Report.pdf, p. 163.

10. Vera Institute, *Demographics: How Do Arrest Trends Vary Across Demographic Groups?*, https://arresttrends.vera.org/demographics?, accessed April 16, 2020.

11. US Census Bureau, *Overview of Race and Hispanic Origin: 2010* (March 2011), https://www.census.gov/prod/cen2010/briefs/c2010br-02.pdf, 4.

12. S. E. James et al., *The Report of the 2015 U.S. Transgender Survey* (Washington, DC: National Center for Transgender Equality, 2016), https://www .transequality.org/sites/default/files/docs/USTS-Full-Report-FINAL.PDF, 15, accessed May 20, 2020.

13. Natasha Lennard, "Supreme Court Upholds Trans People's Workplace Protections—but Trans Lives Remain Under Constant Threat," *Intercept*, June 15, 2020, https://theintercept.com/2020/06/15/transgender-rights-supreme -court.

14. Melissa Boteach, Rebecca Vallas, and Eliza Schultz, *A Progressive Agenda to Cut Poverty and Expand Opportunity* (Center for American Progress, June 2016), https://cdn.americanprogress.org/wp-content/uploads/2016/06/03081022 /RoadmapOpportunity-report.pdf, 12.

15. NYC Human Rights, *Gender Identity/Gender Expression: Legal Enforcement Guidance*, https://www1.nyc.gov/site/cchr/law/legal-guidances-gender-identity -expression.page, accessed May 4, 2020.

16. Sylvia Rivera Law Project, *It's War in Here*, https://srlp.org/wp-content /uploads/2012/08/WarinHere042007.pdf, accessed May 20, 2020.

17. Tali Woodward, "Life in Hell: In California Prisons, An Unconventional Gender Identity Can Be Like an Added Sentence," *Women + Prison: A Site for Resistance*, http://womenandprison.org/sexuality/view/life_in_hell_in_california _prisons_an_unconventional_gender_identity_can_be, accessed October 29, 2019.

18. Transgender Law & Policy Institute, "Non-Discrimination Laws That Include Gender Identity and Expression," updated January 2012, http://www .transgenderlaw.org/ndlaws/index.htm.

19. Deborah Sontag, "Transgender Woman Cites Attacks and Abuse in Men's Prison," *New York Times*, April 5, 2015, https://www.nytimes.com/2015/04/06 /us/ashley-diamond-transgender-inmate-cites-attacks-and-abuse-in-mens -prison.html. After suing the Georgia Department of Corrections for failing to provide her with hormone therapy and placing her in men's prisons where she was repeatedly sexually and physically assaulted, Diamond was paroled on August 31, 2015, after serving less than one-third of her sentence.

20. Lori Sexton, Valerie Jenness, and Jennifer Sumner, *Where the Margins Meet: A Demographic Assessment of Transgender Inmates in Men's Prisons*, June 10, 2009, 4, https://www.hivlawandpolicy.org/sites/default/files/A-Demographic -Assessment-of-Transgender-Inmates-in-Mens-Prisons.pdf.

21. Victoria Law, "#MeToo Behind Bars: When the Sexual Assaulter Holds the Keys to Your Cell," *Truthout*, March 18, 2018, https://truthout.org/articles /metoo-behind-bars-when-the-sexual-assaulter-holds-the-keys-to-your -cell.

22. MacArthur Justice Center, "Illinois Dept. of Corrections Moves Trans Woman to Women's Prison," press release, April 3, 2019, https://www .macarthurjustice.org/illinois-dept-of-corrections-moves-trans-woman -to-womens-prison.

23. rseven, "Too Different to Be Recovered," *Daily Kos*, August 3, 2011, https://www.dailykos.com/stories/2011/08/03/1002879/-Too-different -to-be-recovered.

24. Cece McDonald, letter to author, July 19, 2012.

CHAPTER 12: Bringing up a history of abuse and violence is simply an "abuse excuse."

1. American Civil Liberties Union, "Georgetown and ACLU Comment: Proposed Rule, National Standards to Prevent, Detect and Respond to Prison Rape," April 4, 2011, https://www.aclu.org/other/prison-rape-elimination-act-2003 -prea?redirect=prisoners-rights-womens-rights/prison-rape-elimination -act-2003-prea.

2. While this chapter examines the abuse-to-prison pipeline for girls and women, I want to acknowledge that boys and men who end up in the prison system also experience histories of abuse. A 1999 Department of Justice study on abuse and incarceration found that, among people in men's state prisons, 16 percent reported being physically and/or sexually abused prior to their incarceration. (The study does not clarify whether all respondents were men or if some transgender women in men's prisons were included in the study.) Catherine Wolf Harlow, *Prior Abuse Reported by Inmates and Probationers* (Washington, DC: Bureau of Justice Statistics, April 1999), https://www.bjs.gov/content/pub/pdf /parip.pdf.

3. *Domestic Violence Homicide in Oklahoma: A Report of the Oklahoma Domestic Violence Fatality Review Board* (Domestic Violence Fatality Review Board, 2015), http://www.oag.ok.gov/Websites/oag/images/Documents/Divisions/Victim%20 Services/Domestic_Violence_Fatality_Review_Board_Annual_Report_2015.pdf, 5.

4. Mary Fish, letter to the author, July 30, 2019.

5. Elizabeth Swavola, Kristina Riley, and Ram Subramanian, *Overlooked: Women and Jails in an Era of Reform* (Vera Institute of Justice, 2016), https:// storage.googleapis.com/vera-web-assets/downloads/Publications/overlooked -women-and-jails-report/legacy_downloads/overlooked-women-and-jails -report-updated.pdf, 11.

6. *Female Homicide Commitments: 1986 vs. 2005*, New York State Department of Correctional Services, 2007, https://doccs.ny.gov/system/files/documents /2019/09/Female_Homicide_Commitments_1986_vs_2005.pdf, 14.

7. Tamar Kraft-Stolar, E. Brundige, S. Kalantry, J. G. Kestenbaum, *From Protection to Punishment: Post-Conviction Barriers to Justice for Domestic Violence Survivor-Defendants in New York State*, Correctional Association of New York, 2011, http://scholarship.law.cornell.edu/avon_clarke/2.

8. Victoria Law, "Freeing Marissa Alexander," *Truthout*, October 16, 2013, https://truthout.org/articles/freeing-marissa-alexander/#ixzz2284CoqHb.

9. Victoria Law, "Awareness of the Criminalization of Survivors Is Increasing—Has It Entered Courtrooms?" *Truthout*, June 4, 2017, https://truthout.org /articles/awareness-of-the-criminalization-of-survivors-is-increasing-has-it -entered-the-courtroom.

10. Victoria Law, "Why Is California Keeping Kelly Savage in Prison for a Crime She Didn't Commit?," *Truthout*, November 29, 2014, https://truthout.org /articles/why-is-california-keeping-kelly-savage-in-prison-for-a-crime-she -didn-t-commit. In 2017 California governor Jerry Brown commuted her sentence, making her eligible for parole. She was granted parole and released in November 2018.

11. Alex Campbell, "This Battered Woman Wants to Get Out of Prison," *BuzzFeed News*, November 11, 2014, https://www.buzzfeednews.com/article/alex campbell/this-battered-woman-wants-to-get-out-of-prison.

12. State of Oklahoma v. Robert Braxton and Tondalo Hall, No. CF2004-6403, October 5, 2006, https://www.documentcloud.org/documents/1338621-tondalo -hall-documents.html#document/p32/a186114.

13. Stephanie K. Baer, "A Battered Woman Who Was Imprisoned for 15 Years for Failing to Protect Her Kids from Abuse Has Been Freed," *Buzzfeed News*, November 8, 2019, https://www.buzzfeednews.com/article/skbaer/tondalo -hall-abuse-release-prison-oklahoma.

14. Figures provided by Rachel White-Domain, an attorney with Cabrini Green Legal Aid, October 3, 2019.

15. Victoria Law, "When Abuse Victims Commit Crimes," *Atlantic*, May 21, 2019, https://www.theatlantic.com/politics/archive/2019/05/new-york -domestic-violence-sentencing/589507.

16. Victoria Law, "Domestic Violence Victims in NY Prisons May Get Some Relief," *Al Jazeera America*, January 1, 2015, http://america.aljazeera.com/articles /2015/1/1/domestic-violencevictimsinnyprisonsmaygetsomerelief.html.

17. Patrick Lakamp, "'Epitome of a Domestic Violence Victim' or Not, She's Still Going to Prison," *Buffalo News*, September 8, 2019, https://buffalonews.com /2019/09/08/her-lawyer-called-her-epitome-of-a-domestic-violence-victim -but-shes-still-going-to-prison.

18. Holly Krig, "How We Get Free: An Organizing Story and a Love Letter," *Truthout*, February 15, 2018, https://truthout.org/articles/how-we-get-free-an -organizing-story-and-a-love-letter.

CHAPTER 13: Mass incarceration and immigrant detention are unrelated issues that can be addressed separately.

1. Malik Ndaula and Debbie Satyal, "Rafiu's Story: An American Nightmare," in *Keeping Out the Other: A Critical Introduction to Immigration Enforcement Today*, ed. David C. Brotherton and Philip Kretsedemas (New York: Columbia University Press, 2008), 241, 250.

2. J. Rachel Reyes, *Virtual Brief: Immigration Detention: Recent Trends and Scholarship*, Center for Migration Studies, March 26, 2018, https://cmsny.org /publications/virtualbrief-detention.

3. The term "crimmigration," which refers to the intersections of policing and immigration, was coined in 2006 by legal scholar Julie Stump. It was popularized by migration scholar and University of Denver law professor César

Cuauhtémoc García Hernández, who has been writing about this nexus since 2009 on his blog at http://crimmigration.com.

4. Guillermo Cantor, Mark Noferi, and Daniel E. Martinez, Executive Summary, *Special Report: Enforcement Overdrive: A Comprehensive Assessment of ICE's Criminal Alien Program* (American Immigration Council, November 2015), http://immigrationpolicy.org/research/enforcement-overdrive-comprehensive-assessment-ice%E2%80%99s-criminal-alien-program.

5. Seth Freed Wessler, "'This Man Will Almost Certainly Die,'" *Nation*, January 28, 2016, https://www.thenation.com/article/archive/privatized-immigrant-prison-deaths.

6. Detention Management, Immigration and Customs Enforcement, Detention Statistics tab, https://www.ice.gov/detention-management, accessed October 21, 2019.

7. American Civil Liberties Union, letter to Cameron Quinn and John Roth of the Department of Homeland Security, September 26, 2017, updated November 13, 2017, https://www.americanimmigrationcouncil.org/sites/default/files/general_litigation/complaint_increasing_numbers_of_pregnant_women_facing_harm_in_detention.pdf.

8. Liz Jones, "Pregnant and Detained," *All Things Considered*, National Public Radio, April 6, 2018, https://www.npr.org/2018/04/05/599802820/pregnant-and-detained.

9. *Private Prisons in the United States* (Sentencing Project, October 24, 2019), https://www.sentencingproject.org/publications/private-prisons-united-states/.

10. Carl Takei, Michael Tan, and Joanne Lin, "Shutting Down the Profiteers: Why and How the Department of Homeland Security Should Stop Using Private Prisons," white paper, American Civil Liberties Union, September 2016, https://www.aclu.org/sites/default/files/field_document/white_paper_09-30-16_released_for_web-v1-opt.pdf.

11. "Intergovernmental Service Agreement between the United States Department of Homeland Security US Immigration and Customs Enforcement Office of Enforcement and Removal Operations and Karnes County," December 3, 2010, https://www.documentcloud.org/documents/1672377-karnes-county-tx-geo-group-igsa-contract.html#document/p4/a221318; "US Immigration and Customs Enforcement Budget Overview," Fiscal year 2020, Department of Homeland Security, https://www.dhs.gov/sites/default/files/publications/19_0318_MGMT_CBJ-Immigration-Customs-Enforcement_0.pdf.

12. See chapter 15 for more about the resistance actions of women incarcerated in Basile during that time.

13. Auditi Guha, "'Complicit' New Jersey Democrats Face Pressure to End ICE Contracts," *Rewire News*, July 12, 2019, https://rewire.news/article/2019/07/12/complicit-new-jersey-democrats-face-pressure-to-end-ice-contracts.

14. Guha, "'Complicit' New Jersey Democrats."

15. "Transfers of ICE Detainees from the Baldwin County Corrections Center, TRAC Immigration, 2016, https://trac.syr.edu/immigration/detention/201509/BALDWAL/tran.

16. Project South, Letter to Georgia Congressional Delegates, October 17, 2019, https://projectsouth.org/wp-content/uploads/2019/10/10.17.2019-Letter-to-Georgia-Congressional-Delegates-.pdf.

17. Project South, Letter to Georgia Congressional Delegates; Ashton Blatz, "Migrants in ICE's Trans Unit Describe Dire Conditions, Beg for Help," *Advocate*, July 17, 2019, https://www.advocate.com/transgender/2019/7/17/migrants-ices-trans-unit-describe-dire-conditions-beg-help.

18. Project South, Letter to Georgia Congressional Delegates.

19. Danielle Bennett (ICE spokeswoman), email to author, May 17, 2018.

20. Victoria Law, "Investigation: Corporations Are Profiting from Immigrant Detainees' Labor. Some Say It's Slavery," *In These Times*, May 29, 2018, http://inthesetimes.com/features/ice_immigrant_detention_centers_forced_prison_labor_investigation.html.

CHAPTER 14: Most people are in prison for nonviolent drug offenses. Let them out and we'll end mass incarceration.

1. Mary Fish, phone interview, September 18, 2019.

2. Victoria Law, "Why Are So Many Women Behind Bars in Oklahoma?," *Nation*, September 29, 2015, https://www.thenation.com/article/why-are-so-many-women-behind-bars-in-oklahoma.

3. Carson, *Prisoners in 2018*, Tables 13 and 14.

4. Carson, *Prisoners in 2018*, Tables 13 and 14.

5. Cohen, *Prisoners in 1990*; Beck and Harrison, *Prisoners in 2000*.

6. "A Primer: Three Strikes—The Impact After More Than a Decade," Legislative Analyst's Office, October 2005, https://lao.ca.gov/2005/3_strikes/3_strikes_102005.htm.

7. "Good Riddance to Bad Law: 10-20-LIFE," editorial, *Miami Herald*, https://www.miamiherald.com/opinion/editorials/article62557122.html, accessed April 10, 2020.

8. Yawu Miller, "SJC Justice Backs Rollins in Spat with Judge," *Bay State Banner*, September 11, 2019, https://www.baystatebanner.com/2019/09/11/sjc-justice-backs-rollins-in-spat-with-judge.

9. Erik Eckholm, "Out of Prison, and Staying Out, After 3rd Strike in California," *New York Times*, February 26, 2015, https://www.nytimes.com/2015/02/27/us/california-convicts-are-out-of-prison-after-third-strike-and-staying-out.html.

10. Less than half (82,000 of 174,000) of people in federal prisons have been convicted for drug offenses. Only 15 percent (200,000) of the 1.3 million people in state prisons are there because of drug laws. Wagner and Sawyer, *Mass Incarceration*.

11. Victoria Law, "Betsy Ramos' Abusive Boyfriend Killed a Cop. She Has Been Locked Up for 21 Years," *Filter*, January 3, 2019, https://filtermag.org/2019

/01/03/betsy-ramos-abusive-boyfriend-killed-a-cop-she-has-been-locked
-up-for-21-years.

12. Stephanie S. Covington, "Women and Addiction: A Trauma-Informed
Approach," *Journal of Psychoactive Drugs*, November 2008, https://www.stephanie
covington.com/assets/files/CovingtonSARC5.pdf.

13. Cathy Burke, "Released Thugs Have Long, Violent Record," *New York Post*,
January 6, 1999, https://nypost.com/1999/01/06/released-thugs-have-long
-violent-record; Steve Dunleavy, "So Where Are the Tears for This Brave Hero?,"
New York Post, March 2, 1999, https://nypost.com/1999/03/02/so-where-are
-the-tears-for-this-brave-hero.

CHAPTER 15: **People in prison don't resist or organize against abusive conditions.**

1. "Attica Prison Liberation Faction, Manifesto of Demands 1971," Lib.com,
January 6, 2012, https://libcom.org/blog/attica-prison-liberation-faction
-manifesto-demands-1971-06012012.

2. Victoria Law, "Tens of Thousands of California Prisoners Launch Mass
Hunger Strike," *Nation*, July 10, 2013, https://www.thenation.com/article/tens
-thousands-california-prisoners-launch-mass-hunger-strike.

3. Victoria Law, "'As Long as Solitary Exists, They Will Find a Way to Use It,'"
Nation, July 13, 2018, https://www.thenation.com/article/long-solitary-exists
-will-find-way-use.

4. "Alabama Prison Strike Organizer Speaks from Behind Bars: We Are Engaged in the Struggle for Our Lives," *Democracy Now!*, May 13, 2016, https://www
.democracynow.org/2016/5/13/alabama_prison_strike_organizer_speaks_from.

5. Prisoner Unrest Across the US and Canada, *COVID-19 List of Prisoner
Actions*, https://perilouschronicle.com/covid-19-list-of-prisoner-actions,
accessed May 11, 2020.

6. Sissy, letter to author, September 19, 2016.

7. Jane Cutter, "More Than 30 Immigrant Women on Hunger Strike in NW
Detention Center," *Liberation*, June 23, 2017, https://www.liberationnews.org
/30-immigrant-women-hunger-strike-nw-detention-center.

8. Debbie Nathan, "Immigrant Mothers Are Staging Hunger Strikes to Demand
Calls with their Separated Children," *Intercept*, July 13, 2018, https://theintercept.
com/2018/07/13/separated-children-hunger-strike-immigrant-detention.

9. Debbie Nathan, "Women in ICE Detention, Fearing Coronavirus, Make
Video to Protest Unsafe Conditions," *Intercept*, March 30, 2020, https://the
intercept.com/2020/03/30/coronavirus-ice-detention.

10. Patricia Gagne, *Battered Women's Justice: The Movement for Clemency and
the Politics of Self-Defense* (New York: Twayne Publishers, 1998).

11. This same facility, the South Louisiana Correctional Center, was later
taken over by GEO Group and turned into the ICE detention center where women
staged a video protest during the coronavirus pandemic in 2020.

12. Victoria Law, "Time to Speak Up—Women's Prison Resistance in Alabama," *Waging Nonviolence*, July 15, 2014, https://wagingnonviolence.org
/feature/organizing-hell-womens-prison-resistance-alabama.

13. Law, "Time to Speak Up."

14. Law, "Time to Speak Up."

15. Sissy, letter to author, February 26, 2019.

CHAPTER 16: Prisons keep us safe from murderers and rapists.

1. RAINN (Rape, Abuse and Incest National Network), *The Criminal Justice System: Statistics*, https://www.rainn.org/statistics/perpetrators-sexual-violence, accessed May 6, 2020.

2. Department of Justice, Office of Justice Programs, Bureau of Justice Statistics, *Female Victims of Sexual Violence, 1994–2010*, Table 8, March 2013, https://www.bjs.gov/content/pub/pdf/fvsv9410.pdf.

3. RAINN, *The Criminal Justice System*.

4. RAINN, *The Criminal Justice System*.

5. RAINN, *The Criminal Justice System*.

6. Erica Meiners, *For the Children? Protecting Innocence in a Carceral State* (Minneapolis: University of Minnesota Press, 2016), 58.

7. Ronan Farrow, "From Aggressive Overtures to Sexual Assault: Harvey Weinstein's Accusers Tell Their Stories," *New Yorker*, October 10, 2017, https://www.newyorker.com/news/news-desk/from-aggressive-overtures-to-sexual-assault-harvey-weinsteins-accusers-tell-their-stories; Jan Ransom, "Harvey Weinstein's Stunning Downfall: 23 Years in Prison," *New York Times*, March 11, 2020, https://www.nytimes.com/2020/03/11/nyregion/harvey-weinstein-sentencing.html.

8. Jessica Hopper, "Read the 'Stomach-Churning' Sexual Assault Accusations Against R. Kelly in Full," *Village Voice*, December 16, 2013, https://www.villagevoice.com/2013/12/16/read-the-stomach-churning-sexual-assault-accusations-against-r-kelly-in-full. See also Dream Hampton's 2018 documentary *Surviving R. Kelly*.

9. Elizabeth Hartfield and Theresa Waldrop, "Singer R. Kelly's New York Trial Postponed to September," CNN, April 16, 2020, https://www.cnn.com/2020/04/16/us/r-kelly-new-york-trial-postponed/index.html.

10. Victoria Law, "Almost Every Other Day, a Police Officer Loses Their Badge for Engaging in Sexual Misconduct," *Bitchmedia*, November 3, 2015, https://www.bitchmedia.org/article/year-long-investigation-shows-hundreds-officers-lost-their-badges-rape-sexual-misconduct.

11. Matt Sedensky, "Hundreds of Officers Lose Licenses Over Sexual Misconduct," Associated Press, November 1, 2015, https://apnews.com/fd1d4d05e561462a85abe50e7eaed4ec.

12. Department of Justice, Office of Justice Programs, Bureau of Justice Statistics, National Crime Victimization Survey, 2010–2016 (2017), accessed October 15, 2019.

13. Bureau of Justice Statistics, *Sexual Assault of Young Children as Reported to Law Enforcement: Victim, Incident, and Offender Characteristics* (Department of Justice, Office of Justice Programs, July 2000), 10, https://www.bjs.gov/content/pub/pdf/saycrle.pdf.

14. Martin Kaste, "Open Cases: Why One-Third of Murders in America Go Unresolved," NPR, March 30, 2015, https://www.npr.org/2015/03/30/395069137/open-cases-why-one-third-of-murders-in-america-go-unresolved.

15. Tom Meagher, "Why Are American Cops So Bad at Catching Killers?," Marshall Project, April 2, 2015, https://www.themarshallproject.org/2015/04/02/why-are-american-cops-so-bad-at-catching-killers.

16. Sawyer and Wagner, *Mass Incarceration*.

17. Caroline Wolf Harlow, *Prior Abuse Reported by Inmates and Probationers* (Washington, DC: Bureau of Justice Statistics, April 1999), http://www.bjs.gov/index.cfm?ty=pbdetail&iid=837.

18. Victoria Law, "'The System Abuses Us by Locking Us Up Forever': Aging Survivors Behind Bars," *Truthout*, October 4, 2016, https://truthout.org/articles/the-system-abuses-us-by-locking-us-up-forever-aging-survivors-behind-bars.

19. Liliana Segura, "From Death Row at 16 to Suicide at 45: The Life and Death of Paula Cooper," *Intercept*, June 12, 2015, https://theintercept.com/2015/06/12/paula-cooper-dead-at-45.

20. Two years later, in 2015, Cooper died by suicide.

21. Victoria Law, "Beyond Exonerating the Innocent: Using Storytelling to Humanize Youth Sentenced to Die in Prison," *Truthout*, April 28, 2018, https://truthout.org/articles/beyond-exonerating-the-innocent-using-storytelling-to-humanize-youth-sentenced-to-die-in-prison.

22. "Dylann Roof's Confession, Journal Details Racist Motivation for Church Killings," *Chicago Tribune*, December 10, 2016, https://www.chicagotribune.com/news/nationworld/ct-dylann-roof-charleston-shooting-20161209-story.html.

23. Erik Ortiz, "Dylann Roof, Suspected Charleston Church Shooting Gunman Has Troubled Past," NBC News, June 19, 2015, https://www.nbcnews.com/storyline/charleston-church-shooting/dylann-roof-suspected-charleston-church-shooting-gunman-has-troubled-past-n377686.

CHAPTER 17: Incarceration and sex offender registries are necessary to keep our children safe.

1. National Child Traumatic Stress Network, Child Sexual Abuse Fact Sheet, http://nctsn.org/nctsn_assets/pdfs/caring/ChildSexualAbuseFactSheet.pdf.

2. "Myths and Facts," New York State Division of Criminal Justice Services, April 2014, http://www.criminaljustice.ny.gov/nsor/som_mythsandfacts.htm.

3. Bushra Rehman, "Secret Survivor: An Interview with Amita Swadhin," Feminist Wire, October 21, 2012, https://thefeministwire.com/2012/10/secret-survivor-an-interview-with-amita-swadhin.

4. Joan Tabachnick and Alisa Klein, *A Reasoned Approach: Reshaping Sex Offender Policy to Prevent Child Sexual Abuse* (Association for the Treatment of Sexual Abusers, 2011), 19, http://www.atsa.com/pdfs/ppReasonedApproach.pdf.

5. Mimi Kim et al., "Plenary 3—Harms of Criminalization and Promising Alternatives (Transcript)," *University of Miami Race & Social Justice Law Review* 5,

no. 2 (July 2015): 370, https://repository.law.miami.edu/cgi/viewcontent
.cgi?referer=https://www.google.com/&httpsredir=1&article=1045&context
=umrsjlr.

6. Tabachnick and Klein, *A Reasoned Approach*, 22.

7. Tabachnick and Klein, *A Reasoned Approach*, 22.

8. Kim et al., "Plenary 3—Harms of Criminalization," 375–76.

9. Tabachnick and Klein, *A Reasoned Approach*, 33.

10. Tabachnick and Klein, *A Reasoned Approach*, 2.

11. Tabachnick and Klein, *A Reasoned Approach*, 2.

12. Chanakya Sethi, "The Ridiculous Laws That Put People on the Sex Offender List," *Slate*, August 12, 2014, https://slate.com/news-and-politics/2014
/08/mapped-sex-offender-registry-laws-on-statutory-rape-public-urination
-and-prostitution.html.

13. Adam H. Johnson, "The Appeal Podcast: The Rise of Registries," Appeal,
September 12, 2019, https://theappeal.org/the-appeal-podcast-the-rise-of
-registries.

14. Sethi, "The Ridiculous Laws That Put People on the Sex Offender List."

15. Robert Barnoski, *Sex Offender Sentencing in Washington State: Has Community Notification Reduced Recidivism?*, Washington State Institute for Public
Policy, 2005.

16. Emily Horowitz, *Protecting Our Kids? How Sex Offender Laws Are Failing Us*
(Santa Barbara, CA: Praeger), 94.

17. Horowitz, *Protecting Our Kids?*, 118.

18. Grant Duwe, William Donnay, and Richard Tewksburg, "Does Residential Proximity Matter? A Geographic Analysis of Sex Offense Recidivism,"
Criminal Justice and Behavior 35, no. 4 (2008): 484–504.

19. Horowitz, *Protecting Our Kids?*, 42.

20. Tabachnick and Klein, *A Reasoned Approach*, 26–27.

21. Tabachnick and Klein, *A Reasoned Approach*, 26.

22. Tabachnick and Klein, *A Reasoned Approach*, 30.

23. *Hollow Water*, dir. Bonnie Dickie (Mid-Canada Production Services,
2000), National Film Board, Canada, https://www.nfb.ca/film/hollow_water.

24. *Hollow Water*.

25. J. Tabachnick and E. Dawson, "Stop It Now! Vermont: A Four-Year
Program Evaluation (1995–1999)," *Offender Programs Report* 1, no. 4 (October–
November 2000): 49.

CHAPTER 18: The system is broken and we simply need some reforms to fix it.

1. Five of the nine commutations Brown issued in August 2017 were for
those sentenced to LWOP. "California Governor Commutes Nine Lengthy Prison
Sentences," *U.S. News and World Report*, August 18, 2018, https://www.usnews
.com/news/best-states/california/articles/2017-08-18/california-governor
-commutes-9-lengthy-prison-sentences. In November 2018, 32 of Brown's
70 commutations were to those serving LWOP; in December, 73 of Brown's 131

Christmas Eve commutations had been serving LWOP. Bob Egelko, "Governor Jerry Brown Sets Record for Pardons and Commutations in California," *San Francisco Chronicle*, updated December 26, 2018, https://www.sfchronicle.com /politics/article/Gov-Jerry-Brown-sets-record-for-pardons-13487741.php.

2. Dennis Slattery, "Gov. Cuomo Grants Clemency to Abused Upstate Woman Convicted of Murder as Advocates Call for More Action," *New York Daily News*, January 3, 2020, https://www.nydailynews.com/news/politics/ny-cuomo -pardons-commutations-20200104-ixqvtjerxfanxeog4sujz2wjc4-story.html; Victoria Law, "Why It Matters That an Imprisoned Domestic Violence Survivor Was Granted Clemency," *Nation*, January 23, 2017, https://www.thenation.com /article/archive/why-it-matters-that-an-imprisoned-domestic-violence -survivor-was-granted-clemency.

3. When these debates were happening in 2019, New York City jails held approximately 8,000 people. In May 2020, due in large part to bail reform and advocacy efforts in the face of COVID-19, that number had dropped to 3,900.

4. Victoria Law, "After Seven Long Years, Freedom: An Interview with Marissa Alexander," *Truthout*, March 13, 2017, https://truthout.org/articles/after -seven-long-years-freedom-an-interview-with-marissa-alexander.

5. Stephanie Fahy et al., "Use of Electronic Offender-Tracking Devices Expands Sharply," Pew Charitable Trusts, September 7, 2016, www.pewtrusts.org /en/research-and-analysis/issue-briefs/2016/09/use-of-electronic-offender -tracking-devices-expands-sharply.

6. Matt Masterson, "'We Reached That Limit': Cook County Sheriff Out of Electronic Monitoring Equipment," WTTW, May 7, 2020, accessed May 16, 2020, https://news.wttw.com/2020/05/07/we-reached-limit-cook-county-sheriff -out-electronic-monitoring-equipment.

7. James Kilgore, "Let's Fight for Freedom from Electronic Monitors and E-Carceration," *Truthout*, September 4, 2019, https://truthout.org/articles /lets-fight-for-freedom-from-electronic-monitors-and-e-carceration.

8. Ruth Wilson Gilmore, *Golden Gulag: Prisons, Surplus, Crisis, and Opposition in Globalizing California* (Berkeley: University of California Press, 2006), 242. The term "non-reformist reform" first appeared in Andre Gorz's 1967 *Strategy for Labor*. Gorz defined it as "one which is conceived not in terms of what is possible within the framework of a given system or administration, but in view of what should be made possible in terms of human needs and demands."

CHAPTER 19: We should make our prisons more like those in Norway.

1. Kim Ekhaugen, Colette S. Peters, and Jordan M. Hyatt, "The Nordic Model: Norway's Penal Reform, Scandinavia House," panel discussion, Scandinavia House Cultural Programs, September 18, 2019.

2. Baz Dreisinger, *Incarceration Nations: A Journey to Justice in Prisons around the World* (New York: Other Press, 2016), 273.

3. Victor L. Shammas, "The Rise of a More Punitive State: On the Attenuation of Norwegian Penal Exceptionalism in an Era of Welfare State

Transformation," August 2015, 64, https://static1.squarespace.com/static
/5a8d8d5c8obd5e24bco797f6/t/5ab2cob3o3ce646492029950/1521664180824
/Shammas_V._L._2016_The_rise_of_a_more_pu.pdf.

4. Dreisinger, *Incarceration Nations*, 278.

5. Ekhaugen, Peters, and Hyatt, "The Nordic Model."

6. Vince Bzdek, "New Prisons Chief Wants to Correct Corrections," *Colorado Springs Gazette*, October 19, 2019, https://gazette.com/news/new-prisons-chief-wants-to-correct-corrections/article_46e5120a-f220-11e9-b268-8779d82d18od.html.

7. World Prison Brief, "Norway," https://www.prisonstudies.org/country/norway, accessed April 12, 2020.

8. Sivilombudsmannen, Norwegian Parliamentary Ombudsman, *Women in Prison: A Thematic Report About the Conditions for Female Prisoners* (December 2016), https://www.sivilombudsmannen.no/wp-content/uploads/2017/05/SIVOM_temarapport_ENG_WEB_FINAL.pdf.

9. Sivilombudsmannen, *Women in Prison*; Ekhaugen, Peters, and Hyatt, "The Nordic Model."

10. Ekhaugen, Peters, and Hyatt, "The Nordic Model."

11. Shammas, "Rise of a More Punitive State," 73–74.

12. Thomas Ugelvik, "The Limits of the Welfare State? Foreign National Prisoners in the Norwegian Crimmigration Prison," in *Scandinavian Penal History, Culture and Prison Practice: Embraced by the Welfare State?*, ed. Peter Scharff Smith and Thomas Ugelvik (London: Palgrave MacMillan, 2017), 413–14.

13. Victor L. Shammas, "Prisons of Labor: Social Democracy and the Triple Transformation of the Politics of Punishment in Norway, 1900–2014," in Smith and Ugelvik, *Scandinavian Penal History, Culture and Prison Practice*, 72.

14. Shammas, "Rise of a More Punitive State," 75.

15. Some advocates estimate that the number could be as high as two hundred thousand or even higher, but the lack of transparency around monitoring means that an exact total remains unavailable.

16. Shammas, "The Rise of a More Punitive State," 65.

17. Siobhan O'Grady, "European Court Rejects Mass Murderer Anders Breivik's Claim That Isolation in Three-Room Cell Is Inhumane," *Washington Post*, June 21, 2018, https://www.washingtonpost.com/news/worldviews/wp/2018/06/21/european-court-rejects-mass-murderer-anders-breiviks-claim-that-isolation-in-three-room-cell-is-inhumane.

18. "Killer Anders Breivik Makes Nazi Salute in Court Case over Jail Cell," NBC News, March 15, 2016, https://www.nbcnews.com/news/world/killer-anders-breivik-makes-nazi-salute-court-case-over-jail-n538521.

19. Victor L. Shammas, "The Pains of Freedom: Assessing the Ambiguity of Scandinavian Penal Exceptionalism on Norway's Prison Island," *Punishment & Society* 16, no. 1 (2014): 107, 117, https://static1.squarespace.com/static/5a8d8d5c8obd5e24bco797f6/t/5ab2coe4575d1f8c594a22f1/1521664228946/Shammas_V._L._2014_The_pains_of_freedom.pdf.

20. Casey Tolan, "Inside the Most Humane Prison in the World, Where Inmates Have Flatscreen TVs and Cells are Like Dorms," *Splinter*, September 14, 2016, https://splinternews.com/inside-the-most-humane-prison-in-the -world-where-inmat-1793861894.

21. Ekhaugen, Peters, and Hyatt, "The Nordic Model."

CHAPTER 20: Prisons are the only logical and evident way to address violent crime and meet the needs of victims.

1. Erika Harrell, *Black Victims of Violent Crime*, Special Report (Washington, DC: Bureau of Justice Statistics, August 2007), 3, https://www.bjs.gov/content /pub/pdf/bvvc.pdf; Karen F. Parker, *Unequal Crime Decline: Theorizing Race, Urban Inequality, and Criminal Violence* (New York: New York University Press, 2008).

2. Danielle Sered, *Young Men of Color and the Other Side of Harm: Addressing Disparities in Our Responses to Violence* (Vera Institute of Justice, December 2014), https://storage.googleapis.com/vera-web-assets/downloads/Publications/young -men-of-color-and-the-other-side-of-harm-addressing-disparities-in-our -responses-to-violence/legacy_downloads/men-of-color-as-victims-of -violence-v3.pdf.

3. Amanda Winkler, "A Mother's Wish for Her Son's Killer," Freethink, April 17, 2019, https://www.freethink.com/articles/alternatives-to-incarceration -building-a-survivor-centered-justice-system.

4. "Restorative Justice and Prison Reform, Part II," June 2, 2019, *Paradigms*, podcast, https://paradigms.life/2019/restorative-justice-and-prison-reform -pt-ii.

5. "Until We Reckon: Mass Incarceration, Violence and the Radical Possibilities of Restorative Justice," *Democracy Now!*, March 14, 2019, https://www .democracynow.org/2019/3/14/until_we_reckon_mass_incarceration_violence.

6. Emily Yoffe, "Innocence Is Irrelevant," *Atlantic*, September 2017, https:// www.theatlantic.com/magazine/archive/2017/09/innocence-is-irrelevant /534171.

7. Michelle Alexander, "Reckoning with Violence," editorial, *New York Times*, March 3, 2019, https://www.nytimes.com/2019/03/03/opinion/violence -criminal-justice.html.

8. Public News Service, *Report: Restorative Justice for Juveniles Works Better Than Jail Time* (May 2019), https://www.publicnewsservice.org/2019-05-30 /juvenile-justice/report-restorative-justice-for-juveniles-works-better-than -jail-time/a66625-1.

9. sujatha baliga, Sia Henry, and Georgia Valentine, *Restorative Community Conferencing: A Study of Community Works West's Restorative Justice Youth Diversion Program in Alameda County* (Impact Justice, Summer 2017), https://impactjustice .org/wp-content/uploads/CWW_RJreport.pdf.

10. "35 States Encourage Restorative Justice as Prison Alternative," *Crime and Justice News* (July 20, 2016), https://thecrimereport.org/2016/07/20/35 -states-encourage-restorative-justice-as-prison-alternative.

11. Human Rights Watch, *Justice Compromised: The Legacy of Rwanda's Community-Based Gacaca Courts* (May 2011), https://www.hrw.org/report/2011/05/31/justice-compromised/legacy-rwandas-community-based-gacaca-courts.

12. Human Rights Watch, *Justice Compromised.*

13. Catherine Wambua, "Remembering Rwanda's Genocide," *Al Jazeera*, July 1, 2012, https://www.aljazeera.com/indepth/features/2012/07/201271138234161377.html.

14. Michel Nkurunziza, "Over 149,000 Gacaca Judgements Remain Unexecuted, Say Genocide Survivors' Proponents," *New Times*, May 27, 2019, https://www.newtimes.co.rw/news/over-149000-gacaca-judgements-remain-unexecuted-say-genocide-survivors-proponents.

15. The court granted his appeal on technical grounds, not on the systemic racism argument. Associated Press, "Bill Cosby Granted Right Against Sexual Appeal Conviction," *Guardian*, June 23, 2020, https://www.theguardian.com/world/2020/jun/23/bill-cosby-appeal-granted-sexual-assault-conviction.

16. Mark S. Umbreit, Robert B. Coates, and Betty Vos, "The Impact of Victim-Offender Mediation: Two Decades of Research," *Federal Probation* 65, no. 3 (December 2001); *Scaling Restorative Community Conferencing through a Pay for Success Model: A Feasibility Assessment Report* (National Council on Crime & Delinquency, March 2015), 9; baliga, Henry, and Valentine, *Restorative Community Conferencing*, 6–9.

17. Caroline M. Angel, "Crime Victims Meet Their Offenders: Testing the Impact of Restorative Justice Conferences on Victim's Post-Traumatic Stress Symptoms" (PhD diss., University of Pennsylvania, 2005), https://repository.upenn.edu/dissertations/AAI3165634.

18. Sered, *Until We Reckon*, 143.

CHAPTER 21: Even if societal and political conditions are to blame, there's nothing we can do about it.

1. The Canadian Quaker Ruth Morris, inspired by Native Canadian healing circles and New Zealand's community group conferences as ways to address violence, coined the term "transformative justice" in her book *Stories of Transformative Justice* (Toronto: Canadian Scholars' Press and Women's Press, 2000). It was later popularized by generationFIVE, a Bay Area organization which aimed to end child sexual abuse in five generations.

2. Mia Mingus, "Transformative Justice: A Brief Description," TransformHarm, https://transformharm.org/transformative-justice-a-brief-description, accessed April 12, 2020.

3. Mingus, "Transformative Justice."

4. Sarah Jaffe, "From 'Me Too' to 'All of Us': Organizing to End Sexual Violence," *In These Times*, October 17, 2017, http://inthesetimes.com/article/20613/incarceration-sexual-assault-me-too-rape-culture-organizing-resistance.

5. Alisa Bierria et al., "Taking Risks: Implementing Grassroots Community Accountability Strategies," *The Revolution Starts at Home* (self-published zine),

74, https://www.transformativejustice.eu/wp-content/uploads/2010/11/Taking -Risks.-CARA.pdf, accessed April 16, 2020.

6. Creative Interventions, "Toolkit," http://www.creative-interventions .org/tools/toolkit, accessed April 12, 2020.

7. The zine, published in 2008, is available online at http://criticalresistance .org/wp-content/uploads/2014/05/Revolution-starts-at-home-zine.pdf. The book was originally published in 2011 by South End Press and reprinted in 2016 by AK Press.

8. Mariame Kaba and Shira Hassan, *Fumbling Towards Repair: A Workbook for Community Accountability Facilitators* (Oakland, CA: AK Press, 2019).

9. Ann Russo, *Feminist Accountability: Disrupting Violence and Transforming Power* (New York: New York University Press, 2019), 144–45.

10. Russo, *Feminist Accountability*, 145.

11. "What We Do," NYC Transformative Justice Hub, https://nyctjhub.com /public_whatwedo.html, accessed April 12, 2020. With the spread of coronavirus preventing in-person gatherings, these bimonthly trainings have moved online.

12. Bell Bajao, "Case Study: Breakthrough Campaign Bell Bajao!," http:// www.endvawnow.org/uploads/browser/files/bell_bajao_case_study_english.pdf, accessed April 13, 2020.

13. CMS Communications, *Most Significant Change Stories: A Report* (2009–2010), 10, http://bellbajao.org/wp-content/uploads/2009/06/MSCT-Report -March-8.pdf.

14. "Ruth Rittenhouse Morris: 1933–2001," Quakers in the World, http:// www.quakersintheworld.org/quakers-in-action/162, accessed April 13, 2020.

Index

"Passim" (literally "scattered") indi-
cates intermittent discussion of a
topic over a cluster of pages.

About the Author

Victoria Law is a freelance journalist whose work focuses on the intersections of incarceration, gender, and resistance. She is the author of *Resistance Behind Bars: The Struggles of Incarcerated Women*, coauthor of *Prison By Any Other Name: The Harmful Consequences of Popular Reforms*, and co-editor of *Don't Leave Your Friends Behind: Concrete Ways to Support Families in Social Justice Movements and Communities*. Her writings about incarceration have appeared in various online and print outlets, including the *New York Times*, *The Nation*, *Wired*, *Ms.*, and *Truthout*. She is a cofounder of Books Through Bars–NYC, an all-volunteer program that sends free books to people imprisoned across the country, and was the longtime editor of the zine *Tenacious: Art and Writings by Women in Prison*. She lives in New York City with her daughter.